# Virgin Islands

# WORLD BIBLIOGRAPHICAL SERIES

General Editors:
Robert G. Neville (Executive Editor)
John J. Horton

Robert A. Myers        Ian Wallace
Hans H. Wellisch      Ralph Lee Woodward, Jr.

**John J. Horton** is Deputy Librarian of the University of Bradford and currently Chairman of its Academic Board of Studies in Social Sciences. He has maintained a longstanding interest in the discipline of area studies and its associated bibliographical problems, with special reference to European Studies. In particular he has published in the field of Icelandic and of Yugoslav studies, including the two relevant volumes in the World Bibliographical Series.

**Robert A. Myers** is Associate Professor of Anthropology in the Division of Social Sciences and Director of Study Abroad Programs at Alfred University, Alfred, New York. He has studied post-colonial island nations of the Caribbean and has spent two years in Nigeria on a Fulbright Lectureship. His interests include international public health, historical anthropology and developing societies. In addition to *Amerindians of the Lesser Antilles: a bibliography* (1981), *A Resource Guide to Dominica, 1493–1986* (1987) and numerous articles, he has compiled the World Bibliographical Series volumes on *Dominica* (1987), *Nigeria* (1989) and *Ghana* (1991).

**Ian Wallace** is Professor of German at the University of Bath. A graduate of Oxford in French and German, he also studied in Tübingen, Heidelberg and Lausanne before taking teaching posts at universities in the USA, Scotland and England. He specializes in contemporary German affairs, especially literature and culture, on which he has published numerous articles and books. In 1979 he founded the journal *GDR Monitor*, which he continues to edit under its new title *German Monitor*.

**Hans H. Wellisch** is Professor emeritus at the College of Library and Information Services, University of Maryland. He was President of the American Society of Indexers and was a member of the International Federation for Documentation. He is the author of numerous articles and several books on indexing and abstracting, and has published *The Conversion of Scripts* and *Indexing and Abstracting: an International Bibliography*. He also contributes frequently to *Journal of the American Society for Information Science*, *The Indexer* and other professional journals.

**Ralph Lee Woodward, Jr.** is Chairman of the Department of History at Tulane University, New Orleans, where he has been Professor of History since 1970. He is the author of *Central America, a Nation Divided*, 2nd ed. (1985), as well as several monographs and more than sixty scholarly articles on modern Latin America. He has also compiled volumes in the World Bibliographical Series on *Belize* (1980), *Nicaragua* (1983), and *El Salvador* (1988). Dr. Woodward edited the Central American section of the *Research Guide to Central America and the Caribbean* (1985) and is currently editor of the Central American history section of the *Handbook of Latin American Studies*.

VOLUME 138

# Virgin Islands

Verna Penn Moll

*Compiler*

## CLIO PRESS

OXFORD, ENGLAND · SANTA BARBARA, CALIFORNIA
DENVER, COLORADO

British Library Cataloguing in Publication Data

Moll, Verna Penn
Virgin Islands – (World bibliographical series; v.138)
1. Virgin Islands. Bibliographies
I. Title    II. Series
016.972972

ISBN 1-85109-165-3

Clio Press Ltd.,
55 St. Thomas' Street,
Oxford OX1 1JG, England.

ABC-CLIO,
130 Cremona Drive,
Santa Barbara,
CA 93117, USA.

Designed by Bernard Crossland.
Typeset by Columns Design and Production Services Ltd, Reading, England.
Printed and bound in Great Britain by
Billing and Sons Ltd., Worcester.

# THE WORLD BIBLIOGRAPHICAL SERIES

This series, which is principally designed for the English speaker, will eventually cover every country (and many of the world's principal regions), each in a separate volume comprising annotated entries on works dealing with its history, geography, economy and politics; and with its people, their culture, customs, religion and social organization. Attention will also be paid to current living conditions – housing, education, newspapers, clothing, etc.– that are all too often ignored in standard bibliographies; and to those particular aspects relevant to individual countries. Each volume seeks to achieve, by use of careful selectivity and critical assessment of the literature, an expression of the country and an appreciation of its nature and national aspirations, to guide the reader towards an understanding of its importance. The keynote of the series is to provide, in a uniform format, an interpretation of each country that will express its culture, its place in the world, and the qualities and background that make it unique. The views expressed in individual volumes, however, are not necessarily those of the publisher.

## VOLUMES IN THE SERIES

*In loving memory of Jestina, devoted teacher and medical technician and also of my grandparents, Louisa, Adella, Alicia, Reginald and Joseph*

# Contents

# Contents

## Contents

**Contents**

# Introduction

The Virgin Islands are situated in the Caribbean arc of islands which extends from North to South America, separating the American mediterranean from the Atlantic Ocean. The group forms one ecological system, and consists of seven main islands and over a hundred cays shared between Britain and the United States of America. (Three of the largest islands with an area of 137 square miles and a population of 100,000 are dependencies of the United States; a smaller area – 67 square miles, with 17,733 population (1991 Census) – is under British jurisdiction). The archipelago lies 40 miles east of Puerto Rico between latitudes 17 and 18 degrees north and longitudes 64 and 65 degrees west, and is approximately 3,800 miles from Britain and 1,700 miles from New York.

The group became politically divided during the great 'power play' of the European nations. Since Christopher Columbus came across the islands on 17 November 1493, almost five centuries ago, the Spanish, English, Dutch, French and Danish have all endeavoured to control some or all of the islands (one of them, St. Croix, has changed flags seven times). However, the British have remained in some of them since 1672, chiefly Tortola and Anegada. Denmark annexed St. Thomas in 1692, St. John in 1717 and purchased St. Croix from France in 1733; these three islands were called 'The Danish West Indies'. In 1917 they were purchased from the Danes by the United States of America and renamed the United States Virgin Islands. The others became known as 'The British Virgin Islands'. Thus two distinct political territories were formed.

About the beginning of the 17th century the shift from mere maritime defence to the idea of establishing colonies became a reality. The Danes had developed a robust trading emporium in St.

**Introduction**

Thomas and the English settlers developed a plantation economy in their islands, cotton and sugar being the main products. The war years were periods of great economic prosperity for the islands in the 18th and 19th centuries; trading opportunities were enhanced with the introduction of the Tortola Free Port Act of 1801 and the establishment of a packet station in Road Town, Tortola.

However, the results of the European wars, subsequent peace, and the abolition of slavery all had alarming effects on the rise and fall of both economies. The planters on the British islands left and remaining islanders developed their own forms of small-scale agriculture, boat-building and local industries. St. Thomas had replaced the war trade of earlier periods with the commerce of the Industrial Revolution and was a transhipment point with a coaling station and a depot for great steamship lines. It was an economic saviour for the British islands and for St. John. The metropolitan countries assisted (to a greater or lesser degree) in their colonies, but as the island groups depended on each other for trade and production, economic and social ties grew strong.

In the British Virgin Islands, the mid-20th century was a period of reconstruction, the major occupation being to discover a suitable and effective formula for the economic development of the islands. With the introduction of ministerial government in 1967 and the Development Plan of 1962, the economy started to rise again. A tourist economy was adopted as the resource base, with agriculture and fishing as supporting activities. Some measure of financial independence had been achieved by 1979, when British grant-in-aid was eliminated, but some capital projects are still financed by the British Government and various other overseas aid programmes.

A broader base for investment, linked with an enhanced infrastructure of reliable electrical, telecommunications, transport and water services, is envisaged for the next decade or so, with tourism and off-shore financial services as the bedrock of the economy. The expansion of yachting and marinas, real-estate development and construction, light industries and the distributive trades, has also encouraged the economy. Agriculture, including forestry and fishing, is also being improved (local beef is once more available in supermarkets), with diversification into scientific hydroponics and mariculture.

Financial services expanded as a result of legislative measures adopted in 1984, with a new Company Law in 1990, and following the poltical disturbances in Panama during 1988 and 1989. Over 15,000 International Business Companies were on the register in 1990. The average annual inflation was 1 per cent in 1987 and unemployment is negligible.

The British Virgin Islands have had a representative assembly since 1774, but a new constitution and ministerial government in 1967 brought greater local participation in the welfare and development of the territory. There are three political parties: the Independent People's Movement, the United Party and the Virgin Islands Party. The Lavity Stoutt Government (VIP) held power from 1967 to 1975; the Willard Wheatley Goverment (UP), from 1975 to 1979; the Cyril Romney Government (Independent/United Party coalition) from 1983 to 1986 and from 1986 the Stoutt Government has been again in control. Under the constitution, the Governor, appointed by the Queen, is responsible for defence and internal security, external affairs, terms and conditions of service for public officers and the administration of the courts. Further constitutional revisions and international agreements are assisting progress towards greater self-government and economic growth.

The British Virgin Islands has links with a number of regional bodies, as it seeks to promote economic, trade and social concerns. These include membership of the Caribbean Development Bank (CDB) and the Caribbean Institute of Administration (CARICAD); associate membership of the Organization of Eastern Caribbean States (OECS); and financial support for the University of the West Indies. As a dependency of the United Kingdom, the islands have the status of an Overseas Territory in association with the EEC. However, trade, cultural and family affiliations with the neighbouring United States Virgin Islands are still strong and the US currency has been the sole legal tender in the British Islands since 1965. British Virgin Islands/United States Virgin Islands Friendship Day is observed every November, celebrated in each territory alternately. Official counterparts, service clubs, government departments, professionals and others meet to share concerns in formal discussion and social outings.

The United States Virgin Islands territory, a total of 137 square miles, consists of three main inhabited islands – St. Croix, St. Thomas and St. John, and about forty smaller islands. The capital, Charlotte Amalie, is situated on St. Thomas. The population of 100,000 also enjoys the rights and privileges of full citizenship of the United States of America. Because of their strategic position in relation to the Panama Canal, the Navy Department of America administered the islands until 1931 when management was transferred to the Department of the Interior. They now form an unincorporated territory of the United States of America.

American Virgin Islanders were granted a measure of self-government by an Organic Act of 1936, revised in 1954. This created an elected fifteen-member Senate and since 1970 executive authority has been vested in an elected Governor and Lieutenant-Governor. There are three political parties: the Democratic Party of the Virgin Islands; the Independent Citizens Movement and the Republican Party of the Virgin Islands. Melvin Evans (REP) was Governor from 1970 to 1974; Cyril King (ICM) from 1974 to 1978; Juan Luis also of the Independent Citizens Movement, from 1978 to 1982 and Alexander Farrelly (DP) from 1986 onwards. A constitution which would provide some degree of autonomy has, since 1978, seen several drafts rejected by public referendum. The future status of the islands is still being debated.

Economically the islands are dependent on links with Puerto Rico and the US mainland, with which about 90 per cent of trade is conducted. There are no mineral resources and most goods are imported. Land space is limited for wide-scale cultivation and does not produce sufficient food to satisfy local consumption. However, tax incentives and an agricultural education programme introduced by the extension service of the College of the Virgin Islands, have encouraged the growing of food crops and fruits (see items 341, 352-5, 358). Tourism is the mainstay of the economy and is based on business from visiting cruise ships.

St. Croix has one of the world's largest petroleum refineries, with a capacity of 545,000 barrels per day. Efforts are being made to introduce labour-intensive and non-polluting manufacturing industries. Local rum earns returns from United States excise duty, amounting to about US $40 million per annum.

Since the 1960s, the population of immigrants has grown dramatically; about 40 per cent of the population originates from other Caribbean islands and from mainland USA. Inflation is higher than on the mainland and according to one source, the islands' economy has been in recession since 1981. A prolonged industrial strike in the late 1980s and the devastation caused by Hurricane Hugo have depressed the economy, but it is slowly being revived, especially in the building construction sector.

Before the 15th century three groups of Indians from South America entered the West Indies. The Arawaks settled widely throughout the Virgin Islands as archaeological surveys indicate (see items 103-9). Although these early people vanished after Columbus, their agricultural and boating skills had already influenced the culture. Today, the people are of mixed European and African descent and British Virgin Islanders possess over 37 per cent of the land. In 1984, the British Virgin Islands celebrated 150 years of achievement since emancipation from slavery (see item no. 142).

There is a strong religious tradition in both island groups with over ten active denominations in the British islands alone. There, the

Anglican and Methodist denominations have been at the centre of societal changes in the past; and have laid solid leadership foundations. A Virgin Islands Council of Churches in the British Islands was recently formed to tackle some of the present social ills (see item no. 187).

The culture is a fusion of the various influences the islands have encountered over the years. The Spanish, Dutch, French, English, Africans and, of course, the original Indians have all left their mark. Although modern influences have taken their toll, there is still evidence of heritage in the local fungiband music, the cuisine, the remedies and in the skills of farming, weaving, fishing, boat-building, etc. The August Monday Festival celebrated in the British Virgin Islands during the first week in August and the St. Thomas Carnival celebrated in mid-April each year, reflect the roots of culture in an array of colour, music, food, imagery, mimicry and themes (see items 486, 492).

Theatre and the performing arts flourish in the United States Virgin Islands, assisted by mainland Federal agencies, such as the National Endowment for the Arts, the National Foundation for the Advancement of the Arts, the National Alliance for Arts Education and also several local art organizations. The Reichold Centre for the Arts facilitates the University of the Virgin Islands' programmes of theatre, dance and music and its exhibitions of paintings, printmaking and sculpture; there 'the best of local cultures are exchanged with the best in the world' (see item no. 490).

The British Virgin Islands National Arts Council is defining its rôle and the Public Library has been a leader in encouraging and promoting the arts there (see items 497-8). The Briercliffe Hall, which opened in the early 1980s, facilitates some cultural exchange, and there are useful UNESCO and local recommendations to be adopted (see item no. 489). Despite the fact that the arts are not as developed as they could be, some creative works *have* emerged from among the intelligentsia brought up on Shakespeare, Thomas Hardy, Milton and a heavy diet of the Nelson's *West Indian Reader* classic poem:

> 'There was an Indian who had known no change
> Who strayed content along the sunlit beach gathering
> shells . . .'

Among those Virgin Islands works that will endure are the poems of Sheila Hyndman Wheatley (deceased 1991) which evoke a power both gentle and delightful (see item no. 513).

The introduction of the Community College in 1990 and the hope of reactivating the Extra-mural Department of the University of the West Indies augur well for the future development of the arts.

**Introduction**

In both territories, the local government Archives are under-developed (see items 552-4) and it is to the credit of the Public Library systems in each that so many research materials are accessible. The National Documentation Centre of the British Virgin Islands managed by the Chief Librarian since 1988 is also very useful for the reference facilities there. A documentalist was appointed in 1991.

Both island groups have made tremendous economic and political strides, though not without problems. The most important problems include the effect of drugs and drug trafficking on youth and society, foreign illegal fishing, the depletion of natural resources, and heavy demands on the social services.

The Inter-Virgin Islands conference was reactivated with a new Memorandum of Understanding in 1990, in order to assist in addressing mutually current problems. It was originally established in 1951, as a forum to discuss socio-economic issues between the two governments (including fishing, immigration and labour, health care, trade and transportation) but had lain dormant for several years. High on its agenda is the formulation of an environmental policy in an effort to preserve the islands as a 'precious, natural and psychological resource for humankind' (see item no. 253).

At a time when the New World is divided about whether Columbus was friend or foe and about how he should be remembered at his quincentennial celebrations, this publication is symbolic; it brings together in one volume Virgin Islands materials which tell their story of hardship and struggle, achievement and progress, problems, challenges and aspirations. The bibliography celebrates bonds between the two territories, bonds which transcend Columbus' 'seeds of change' and the ebb and flow of political and economic tides experienced over the past five hundred years.

This work is not exhaustive, but rather endeavours to record the major standard and popular publications written by indigenous and other authors, and to reflect the unique qualities and culture of the islands. It should assist general readers as well as researchers with a special interest in the Virgin Islands.

The scale of development experienced at different times within the Virgin Islands has undoubtedly influenced the output of literature in each. Unlike the British Virgin Islands, the American islands have a long and continuous history of publishing. Several bibliographies have been published, especially of older works (see item no. 48). The first known map of St. Thomas was printed *circa* 1684 and two weekly newspapers, the *St. Thomas Gazette* and the *St. Thomas Monday Advertiser*, began in 1810. The Von Scholten collection of the Enid Baa Public Library in St. Thomas holds an impressive collection of early Virgin Islands materials which attracts scholars and writers worldwide. There is an increasing number of studies and theses about the islands (see item no. 606); several of these are included as main entries and others in the list of theses which appears in the preliminary pages.

The College of the Virgin Islands was established in 1962 to provide readily accessible, good-quality higher education for all residents of the United States Virgin Islands, neighbouring Caribbean islands and other areas as well. The College's community-oriented mission provides outreach programmes for several sectors including government employees, agriculturalists and farmers. The Caribbean Research Institute was established in 1964 to provide serious inquiry and up-to-date research on Caribbean topics. Its publishing output covers histories, technical and special reports on geology, archaeology, ecology, economics, education, energy, the environment, general and micro-state publications (see item no. 479). The college achieved University status in 1986.

The publishing programmes of the Enid Baa Public Library, professional and civic bodies and MAPes MONDe are also contributing significantly. It is regretted that neither the time nor space allotted to this small volume could do justice to such a fertile area of endeavour. However, there is a selective representation of United States Virgin Islands materials including some new and popular items not yet recorded in earlier bibliographies.

Because a comprehensive guide to the literature of the British Virgin Islands has not yet been published, every effort has been made to include the most significant and useful publications of this group. These range from scholarly works and histories to pamphlets and newsletters, covering a wide range of topics. Where no other material on a topic was available, reports on important seminars giving theme, objectives and aims are entered, with addresses from which follow-up informa-tion could be obtained. Government publications which provide up-to-date and realistic information are also included.

Significant among 20th-century books on the British islands by indigenous authors, are the scholarly works of the late Dr Norwell Harrigan and Dr Pearl Varlack, especially the histories and educational studies which have already gained international acclaim (see items 126, 141, 457, 446). Dr Quincey Lettsome has also developed interesting studies in secondary education curricula (see items 439, 456) and Vernon Pickering's histories are popular (see items 120-1). The historical works and professional articles of anthropologist Dr Michael O'Neal (see items 143, 219, 223, 289) and those of lawyer McWelling Todman on economics and related topics are substantial and extremely useful (see items 139, 142, 265, 286, 301). Bertrand Lettsome, a young Conservation Officer, writes with great promise (item no. 385) and teachers, Jennie Wheatley among them, are producing supplementary readers for classroom use (see items 502-3, 506, 509).

Although the main emphasis is on 20th-century works, materials of enduring quality from earlier periods are included, particularly in the History and Travellers' Accounts sections.

The work is arranged for the most part according to the World Bibliographical Series classification system, but the fact that the islands are two distinct political entities undoubtedly also has some bearing on its arrangement. The work is, in effect, two integrated bibliographies.

Tourism has been expanded to highlight its importance to and impact on society and the economy (see items 67-80). Boating (see items 321-6) and fisheries (see items 367-70) reflect the islands' dependence on the sea. Environment and environmental protection emphasize the effort to preserve pristine environmental conditions (see items 384-424). (The British Virgin Islands National Parks Trust is the longest-standing body of its kind in the Eastern Caribbean, and J.R. O'Neal, a founding member, was recently recognized by the United Nations for promoting the planting of trees and for his successful campaigns to establish thirteen parks and protected areas in the territory.) The section on Human Rights calls attention to the need for publication of appropriate documents on a matter which is of increasingly worrying concern.

Each entry in the bibliography has a running number. General Caribbean titles which have relevance to both groups of islands are cited first in each section, followed by the British Virgin Islands entries, followed by those of the United States Virgin Islands. Each sequence in a section is arranged alphabetically as far as possible. There are separate indexes for each of the territories: an author/title index and a subject index. The general items which relate to both groups are entered in the British Virgin Islands indexes with reference numbers in the United States Virgin Islands subject index. General items relating specifically to the United States Virgin Islands are retained there.

*Verna Penn Moll*
*Colchester*
*November 1991*

# Acknowledgements

I have researched Virgin Islands materials for several years but research for this particular work was concentrated in the past two years. In my search, I have made contact with numerous librarians, archivists, historians and Caribbeanists, without whose assistance this work could not have been completed; I am extremely grateful to them all.

Particularly useful collections were: the Public Libraries of the British and United States Virgin Islands; the Ralph Paiwonsky Library of the University of the (United States) Virgin Islands; the Miami Public Library, Florida; the British Library, Reference Division; the Royal Commonwealth Library, London; Afro-Caribbean Collection of Suffolk Public Libraries, UK; the Resources Collection of the Centre for International Briefing, Surrey, UK; the Sloman Collection of the University of Essex, UK. The Colchester Public Library arranged interlibrary loans for me from libraries across Great Britain.

Several individual persons were, however, outstandingly cooperative. They include: British Virgin Islands Chief Librarian Bernadine Louis and her staff who kept me posted with new materials published in the Islands; Nina O'Neal, British Virgin Islands Information Officer; University Librarian David Ottinger, St. Thomas Virgin Islands; and assistant Librarian, Christopher Anderton of the University of Essex. Several Caribbeanists permitted the use of private collections or posted me materials: Michael O'Neal, Ruth Thomas, Enid Baa, Vernon Pickering, Lito Valls, Florence Lewisohn, Quincey Lettsome and various heads of departments who diligently replied to many of my queries; chief among these was Deputy Governor Elton Georges of the British Virgin Islands.

The support and encouragement of my husband, Peter, was unfailing, and to him I am eternally grateful.

# Theses and Dissertations on the Virgin Islands

## Virgin Islands, UK

Hester D. Chisholm. 'A colonial evaluation of the British Leeward Islands and the Virgin Islands of the United States', MA thesis, Clark University, 1938.

N. Harrigan. 'Administration in the British Virgin Islands: a study in retardation', MA thesis, University of Pittsburgh, 1967.

Charles E. Helsley. 'The geology of the British Virgin Islands', PhD thesis, Princeton University, 1960.

Michael O'Neal. 'British Virgin Islands transformations: anthropological perspectives', PhD thesis, Union Graduate School, Ann Arbor, Michigan, 1983. (Available from University Microfilms International, Ann Arbor, Michigan).

Sushila Raghavan. 'Social stratification in Tortola, British Virgin Islands', MA thesis, Brandeis University, 1963.

## Virgin Islands, US

Peter Pardo de Dela. 'The impact of change and political leadership: the case of the United States Virgin Islands', PhD dissertation, Tulane University, 1978.

Thomas W. Donnelly. 'The geology of St. Thomas and St. Johns, Virgin Islands', PhD dissertation, Princeton University, 1959.

Margaret Allison Gibson. 'Ethnicity and schooling: a Caribbean case study', PhD dissertation, University of Pittsburgh, 1976.

James Green. 'Social networks in St. Croix, United States Virgin Islands', PhD thesis, University of Washington, 1972.

S. Jones-Hendrickson. 'The dynamics of the labour market for nurses from the Commonwealth Caribbean', PhD dissertation, University of Exeter, 1976.

Hazel M. McFerson. 'The impact of a changed racial tradition: race politics and society in the United States Virgin Islands – 1917-1975', PhD dissertation, Brandeis University, 1975.

Patricia Gill Murphy. 'The education of new blacks in the Danish West Indies/United States Virgin Islands: a case study of social transition', PhD dissertation, University of Connecticut, 1977.

Ezra A. Naughton. 'The origin and development of higher education in the Virgin Islands', PhD dissertation, Catholic University of America, 1973.

Martin G. Orlins. 'The impact of tourism on the Virgin Islands of the United States', PhD dissertation, Columbia University, 1969.

Whitney T. Perkins. 'American policy in the government of its dependent areas – a study of the policy of the United States towards the inhabitants of its territories and insular possessions', PhD dissertation, Fletcher School of Law and Diplomacy, 1948.

Pauline Holman Pope. 'Cruzan slavery: an ethnohistorical study of differential responses to slavery in the West Indies', PhD dissertation, University of California, 1969.

Charles Wesley Turnbull. 'The structural development of a public educational system in the Virgin Islands, 1917-1970: a functional analysis in historical perspective', PhD dissertation, University of Minnesota, 1976.

Lionel Vallee. 'The negro family on St. Thomas: a study of role differention', PhD dissertation, Cornell University, 1964.

Waldemar Westergaard. The Danish West Indies under company rule – 1754', PhD dissertation, University of California, 1917.

Jean Louise Willis. 'The trade between North America and the Danish West Indies, 1756-1807, with special reference to St. Croix', PhD dissertation, Columbia University, 1963.

# The Islands and Their Peoples

## General

1 **The Caribbean, Bermuda and the Bahamas 1991.**
Stephen Birnbaum, Alexander Birnbaum.   Boston, Massachussets:
Houghton Mifflin, 1990. 974p. maps.
A general guide which provides a glimpse of special places on each island in the region,
and directs readers to other sources as well as providing information about the best
hotels. The British Virgin Islands appear on pages 366-83 and the United States Virgin
Islands on pages 851-82.

2 **Caribbean handbook, 1986.**
Edited by Jeremy Taylor.   St. Johns, Antigua: F.T. Caribbean, 1986.
224p. maps.
The editorial introduction focuses on general West Indian history, banking,
telecommunications, Caribbean Community (CARICOM), currencies and tourism.
Country-by-country summaries are provided, including those for the British Virgin
Islands on pages 63-8 and the United States Virgin Islands on pages 205-9.

3 **Caribbean: the Lesser Antilles.**
Edited by David Schwab.   Singapore: APA, 1989. 373p. (Insight
Guides).
The guide covers all the islands in the Lesser Antilles group and provides information
on communication, holidays, accommodation and activities in each. Pages 94-105 deal
with the British Virgin Islands; pages 80-91 cover the United States Virgin Islands.

1

4   **The Commonwealth year book, 1990.**
Commonwealth Secretariat.   London: HMSO, 1990. 539p. map.
A compendium of information about the geography, climate, communications, economics, history and constitution of countries in the Commonwealth. The Virgin Islands section on pages 418-25 is very up-to-date.

5   **Penguin guide to the Caribbean.**
Edited by Alan Tucker.   Harmondsworth, England: Penguin, 301p. maps.
Describing the country, major interests, towns and hotels, Susan Farewell writes a very warm and friendly introduction to the Virgin Islands on pages 89-104 and 105-17.

6   **Statesman's year book, 1990-91.**
Edited by John Paxton.   London: Macmillan, 1990. 1689p. maps.
This is a one-volume encyclopaedia with statistical and historical annual information about every state in the world. The Virgin Islands are well represented on pages 30 and 1591-2.

7   **The West Indian islands.**
George Hunte.   London: Batsford, 1972. 146p. 9 maps. bibliog.
Hunte focuses on the general prehistory and history of the region. He examines the impact of tourism, arts, crafts, folklore and the problem of Caribbean identity, all of which are particularly relevant in the Virgin Islands where tourism is the main industry.

# Virgin Islands, UK

8   **The beautiful British Virgin Islands.**
Arnold Highfield.   Road Town, Tortola: Spectra Graphics for Island Services (BVI), 1972. 32p. bibliog.
This booklet highlights some of the best features of the islands: the climate, culture, buildings and people. It gives just enough information to stimulate further interest.

9   **British Virgin Islands: territorial report for the year 1987.**
Office of the Governor.   Road Town, Tortola: British Virgin Islands Government, 1988. 79p. map. bibliog.
This annual up-to-date source of information about the territory was originally published by Her Majesty's Stationery Office (HMSO) in London. It has appeared under various titles, for example, Colonial Year Books: Biannual reports. Part 1 gives a general review of the economy, politics and constitution, society, culture and social services. Part 2 deals with geography and land-use planning; part 3 with population and labour; part 4 reviews the economy; part 5 details the infrastructure and communications; part 6 outlines the social serivces and part 7 deals with other services, such as the police, prison and fire and rescue service. There are appendixes with statistics on

disease, health, population and crime. It is to be regretted that, according to information received from the Deputy Governor's Office, a later edition of such a useful source had not yet been published when we went to press.

## 10 Discover.
Road Town, Tortola: Chief Minister's Office. 1987. 56p.
Published to commemorate the hosting of the eleventh meeting of the Organization of Eastern Caribbean States (OECS), this work is a compendium of the political, social, cultural, educational and developmental aspects of the British Virgin Islands. The articles set the country in its geographical and historical context, and assess social and economic progress in terms of human development and commitment, for the present and in the future. There are significant messages from: Kennedy A. Simmonds, Chairman of the OECS; Vaughan Lewis, Director-General of OECS; Lavity Stoutt, Chief Minister of the British Virgin Islands; and J.M.A. Herdman, Governor. Outstanding articles are 'A destiny to create . . . a nation to mould', by V.P. Moll; 'A historical profile of the British Virgin Islands', by V. Pickering; 'Inter-island trade', by V. Pickering; 'Whither BVI agriculture', by Lorna Smith; 'The National Parks Trust' by N. Clarke; 'National parks: the case for ecodevelopment', by R. Creque; 'Our tourism profile', by Allen O'Neal; 'The organization of the OECS'; 'A look at tourism', by P. Encontre; 'Bareboating in the BVIs', by C. Colli; 'Culture and tourism', by V.A. Brereton; 'Civil aviation in the BVIs' by M. Creque; 'A college for the BVIs', by B. Lewis; 'Overview of education in the BVIs', by C. Wheatley; 'The heritage dancers', by E. Parsons; 'Sports', by B. Penn; 'An observatory in the BVIs', by G. Davis. There are notes on the contributors at the end which add authenticity to this volume.

## 11 A fresh breeze stirs the Leewards.
Carleton Mitchell. *National Geographic*, vol. 130, no. 4 (Oct. 1966), p. 526-37.
The author is obviously very enthusiastic about the colours and people of the British Virgin Islands in this charmingly illustrated article. A number of daily routine activities of Virgin Islanders are described.

## 12 How to retire to the Caribbean.
Sydney Hunt. London: Macmillan, 1989. 164p. map.
Originally published as *How to retire in the British Virgin Islands*, the book has been up-dated and enlarged to cover the needs of the new immigrant population to the islands. It advises on pre-planning, choosing an island, house-building, local customs and the cost of living. With a sprinkling of accents, dialects, patois and recipes, it is very informal and easy to scan.

## 13 Treasure islands: a guide to the British Virgin Islands.
Larry Shepard, Reba Shepard. London; Basingstoke, England: Macmillan, 1989. 144p. maps. bibliog.
An engaging introduction and guide to the British Virgin Islands, this book covers places of interest, marine-orientated activities, historical sights and the cultural heritage. The illustrations are current and informative.

# Virgin Islands, US

14 **People of passion.**
Dana Samuel Orie. St. Thomas: Coral Reef Publications, 1983. 109p.
This chronological selection from the columns of the *Virgin Islands Daily* newspaper from January 1982 to May 1983 gives intimate, yet archetypal experience of the Virgin Islands. Richly illustrated, it shows how 'the search for Caribbean consciousness is being resolved through the merging of Virgin Islands talents'.

15 **Profiles of outstanding Virgin Islanders, vol. 2.**
Coordinated by Ruth Moolenaar. Charlotte Amalie, St. Thomas: Virgin Islands Commission on Youth, 1986. 151p. bibliog.
Provides biographical summaries of Virgin Islanders who have made 'outstanding' contributions to the general welfare of mankind and the development of the islands. The volume is especially intended to develop and strengthen a sense of pride in the Virgin Islands, in the American and Caribbean heritage, and to provide rôle models for students to emulate. Volume 1 was published in 1972 (with 223 pages) and had its second printing in 1976.

16 **The United States Virgin Islands: a charming blend of American and Caribbean cultures.**
Jim Church, Cathy Church. *Skin Diver*, vol. 34 (Jan. 1985), p. 66-85.
A description of the wide range of exciting activities available in the United States Virgin Islands from 'dry' underwater viewing at Coral World to dramatic diving and other beachfront water sports. The article includes a directory of dive operators.

17 **Virgin Islands picture book.**
Antonio Jarvis, Rufus Martin. [n.p.], USA: Dorrance, 1948. 113p.
This combined guide and picture book of the Virgin Islands is now very dated, but it contains sixty-eight illustrations of historical importance. One example is that of the 'public market place' of long ago.

# Geography

## General

18 **Geography for C.X.C.**
Wilma Bailey, Patricia H. Pemberton.   Walton-on-Thames, England:
Nelson, 1983. 154p. maps.
This work is aimed at secondary-school students who are preparing for the Caribbean
Examinations Council (CXC) geography examinations. It deals with topics such as the
physical setting of the Caribbean, sugar, industrialization, transport, communications,
the Caribbean Community (CARICOM) and migration.

19 **Geopolitics of the Caribbean: ministates in a wider world.**
Thomas D. Anderson.   New York: Praeger; Stanford, California:
Hoover Institution Press, 1984. 175p. 8 maps. bibliog.
An overview of the environment and political geography of the region, with much
focus on the Eastern Caribbean including the Virgin Islands. It covers the general
geographical setting, political entities, economic base and historical background. In
addition it deals with marine boundaries and the options for development.

20 **A new geography of the Caribbean.**
Alan Eyre.   London: George Philip, 1962. 162p.
A general survey of the Caribbean region outlining structure, trade and diversity of
population. A brief article on pages 131-2 treats both groups of Virgin Islands,
describing them as a growing tourist resort. There are exercises in practical work and
specimen questions aimed at comprehensive school pupils; suggested studies for sixth-
formers are also included.

21 **Touch the happy isles: a journey through the Caribbean.**
Quentin Crewe. London: Michael Joseph, 1987. 301p.

Unusual in its approach, this work explores the chain of islands from Trinidad to Jamaica, tracing the origins of individuality in landscape, history, art and culture. The author holds discourses with a wide selection of people – from fishermen to prime ministers. Descriptions of the administration, agriculture and tourism of the Virgin Islands appear on pages 209-25 with special reference to Virgin Gorda on pages 216-20 and St. Thomas on pages 214 and 220.

22 **Virgin Islands.**
In: *The international geographic encyclopedia and atlas.* London: Macmillan, 1979, p. 828.

A compact and accurate description of the geography and climate of the islands. The article attributes the current world interest in the islands to the 'tropical climate enhanced by the Old World architecture'. The Virgin Islands National Park in St. John, is also described as being 'rich in marine life, prehistoric Carib indian relics and remains of Danish Colonial sugar plantations'.

# Virgin Islands, UK

23 **The British Virgin Islands: a West Indian anomaly.**
John P. Augelli. *Geographical Review*, vol. 66, vol. 1 (1965), p. 43-56.

A colourful survey of the economic and social conditions of a British territory operating outside the mainstream of the Eastern Caribbean Islands group to which it politically belongs.

24 **Remarks on Anegada.**
Herman Schomburgh. *Journal of Royal Geographical Society*, vol. 2 (1832), p. 152-69.

A first-hand description of Anegada and its reefs, by an author who was travelling in the West Indies when the *Lewis*, an American brig, was wrecked on Anegada. He resolved to re-survey the island and these remarks, with a detailed chart of reefs and soundings between them, were the results of his observations. He also lists the vessels lost on Anegada within living memory.

25 **The Virgins: a descriptive and historical profile.**
Pearl Varlack, Norwell Harrigan. St Thomas: Caribbean Research Institute, 1977. 72p. map. bibliog.

This well-illustrated compendium of geographical description and historical facts treats the politically divided archipelago of islands as a single unit, in recognition of the ecosystem which they form. This represents a unique departure from the traditional approach. Significant facts are presented chronologically and useful information is appended; for example, there are lists of inhabited and uninhabited islands for both

UK and US groups, and demographic statistics from 1691 to 1756. The selected bibliography, which includes articles, increases the value of this ready-reference work.

**Treasure islands: a guide to the British Virgin Islands.**
*See* item no. 13.

**The Virgin Islands story.**
*See* item no. 126.

**A history of the Virgin Islands of the United States.**
*See* item no. 130.

# Geology

## Virgin Islands, UK

26  **Reconnaissance geology of Anegada Island.**
James Howard.   Charlotte Amalie, St. Thomas: Caribbean Research Institute, 1970. 16p. maps.

Howard's findings indicate that 'part of the transition zone between the Puerto Rico Trench and the Caribbean Island arc lies on the northern edge of the Virgin Islands platform'. This northern edge is above water on Anegada Island, on the northernmost projection of the the Virgin Bank. The ages of its low relief and the contrasting high relief of the surrounding islands are determined. The study goes on to show that field-mapping of Anegada and reconnaissance diving on the surrounding reefs suggest that the emergent portion represents the maximum elevation attained by a series of periodically re-established barrier reef–carbonate platform complexes. It is a scientific document of much value.

27  **Reports on the geology of the Leeward and British Virgin Islands.**
P.H.A. Martin-Kaye.   Castries, St. Lucia: Office of the Governor, 1959. 117p. maps.

A detailed analysis of the geology of five countries: Anguilla, Montserrat, Antigua, St. Kitts and the British Virgin Islands. Geological maps and surveys help to clarify the descriptive sections on mineralogy, physical geography, soil sciences and water supplies.

28 **Test well sites and preliminary market evaluation of groundwater potential in Tortola.**
Donald J. Gorgon. San Juan, Puerto Rico: United States Geological Survey, 1966. 35p. maps.

The evaluation was done for the British Virgin Islands in collaboration with the United States Virgin Islands Government. It is an example of the cooperation which exists between the two groups of islands.

29 **Water supplies of the British Virgin Islands.**
P.H.A. Martin-Kaye. Georgetown, British Guiana: Office of the Governor of the Leeward Islands, 1954. 69p.

One of the earliest listings of water supplies in the British Virgin Islands. It was carried out by the geologist of the Leeward Islands, and it records the names of wells and springs, their owners, the year each was sunk, the depth and usage.

# Virgin Islands, US

30 **The effects of rainwater runoff on two undeveloped tropical bays in St. John, United States Virgin Islands.**
Thomas W. Purcell. St. Thomas: Water Resources Centre, Caribbean Research Institute, 1980. 24p. bibliog.

Although the primary aims of the Water Resources Centre are to solve problems of water supply in order to meet demand and to protect the limited water resources of the Virgin Islands, the Centre extends research to include water-related problems and studies. This report shows that while the almost pristine environment is a guarantee against acid-rain pollution, the damage caused by sewerage washed down by rains could be detrimental to the recreational and economic potential of two bays in St. John. Soil brought down from the hills could also contaminate the sea water, affecting the life and growth of bays. The study proposes strategies for collecting and re-routing rain water and also for correcting gutted bays. It is a valuable study, the benefits of which could be applied throughout the tropics.

31 **Geology and ground water resources of St. Croix, Virgin Islands.**
Geological Survey. Washington, DC: United States Printing Office, [n.d.]. 117p.

An important document which identifies the groundwater resources and sets the scene for water resource development in a moderately dry Caribbean island.

32 **Ground water records for St. Croix.**
Hector M. Colon-Ramos. St. Thomas: Caribbean Research Institute, in cooperation with the United States Geological Survey, 1983. 28p.

An authoritative reference source which collates existing water records of the island.

# Climate and hurricanes

## General

33 **Cyclones: Caribbean hurricanes.**
F.C. Farnum.   St. Johns, Antigua: Caribbean Meteorological Institute, 1979. 10p.
An expert hydrometeorologist describes the climatology and related phenomena of Caribbean hurricanes and other natural disasters in the region.

34 **Cyclones: the nature and impact of Hurricane 'Allen'.**
J. Oliver. *Journal of Climatology*, vol. 1 (1981), p. 221-35.
Hurricane Allen, which ravaged the Caribbean in August 1980, is assessed, with the help of many illustrations, tables and diagrams.

35 **Hurricanes: their nature and history, especially those of the West Indies and the southern coast of the United States.**
Ivan R. Tannehill.   Princeton, New Jersey: Princeton University Press, 1938. Reprinted, New York: Greenwood Press, 1969. 157p. maps. bibliog.
Tannehill establishes essential facts about the theories regarding tropical hurricanes in the West Indies and the adjacent waters of the Atlantic Ocean, Gulf of Mexico and Caribbean Sea.

36 **The world weather guide.**
E.A. Pearce, C.G. Smith.   London: Hutchinson, 1984. 480p. bibliog.
A splendid work which describes the weather that can be expected in any part of the world at any given time during the year. The Caribbean is dealt with on pages 315-29. Tables for the islands' weather stations and monthly details of temperature, humidity and precipitation are given.

## Virgin Islands, UK and US

37 **British Virgin Islands national disaster plan.**
National Emergency Advisory Council.   Road Town, Tortola: Office of the Deputy Governor, 1985. 35p.
This document sets out the plan of action to be followed in order to achieve a state of perpetual disaster readiness throughout the territory. It explains the function of each link in the chain of command: from the central committee to communication facilities, home alertness, district contacts, emergency shelters and relief.

38 **Hurricanes in paradise, perception and reality of the hurricane hazard in the Virgin Islands.**
Martyn J. Bowden, Diana Fainberg, Bernard Greenspan, John Shapiro, Stephen Barnhart, Richard Martin, Melvin Noris, Geoffrey Weiner, Richard Kollman.  St. Thomas: Island Resources Foundation, 1974. 115p.

The authors explain the hurricane phenomenon scientifically, but they manage to do so in readable language. They also follow the trail of some historical hurricanes and suggest some forms of readiness which could be introduced. Interesting surveys and questionnaires cover both island groups.

39 **Living through the hell of Hurricane Hugo.**
*Pride*, vol. 7, no. 10 (Oct. 1989), p. 7-15.

The horror and drama of a hurricane that ravaged the islands, told with incredible vividness and force. The photographs help to reinforce the physical impact which Hugo made on the islands, both on the property and on the people.

40 **Trouble in paradise.**
Bernadette Brennan.  *Cruising World.* vol. 11 (Jan. 1985), p. 40-2.

This article describes Hurricane Klaus and the domino effect which it caused, ending in devastation in the Virgin Islands, especially St. Thomas. The illustrations show the force of the wind and waves on boats and harbours.

**A concise history of the British Virgin Islands.**
*See* item no. 120.

**Blue print for paradise: how to live on a tropical island.**
*See* item no. 471.

# Maps and atlases

## General

41 **Macmillan Caribbean certificate atlas.**
London: Macmillan, 1978. 2nd ed. 104p. maps.

The atlas includes maps of the region's physical and political geography and tropical disturbances. The Virgin Islands are mapped.

42 **Wall map of the Caribbean.**
Basingstoke, England: Macmillan, [n.d.].
The map, 850 × 1,220 mm with a scale of 1:3,500,000, was produced in association with the West Indian Committee. It covers basic aspects of regional geography, and includes sea routes and CARICOM membership. The Virgin Islands are included as a large-scale inset.

# Virgin Islands, UK

43 **The British Virgin Islands.**
London: Ministry of Overseas Develpment (Directorate of Overseas Surveys), 1988. 1 sheet. (DOS 997, series 3-OSD).
A small coloured map of the entire group of British Virgin Islands, showing roads, hotels, airports and the boundary line between the British and United States Virgin Islands, on a scale of 1:200,000. There are also six large-scale maps of individual islands (1:25,000): Sheet 1, Jost Van Dyke; Sheet 2, Tortola; Sheet 3, Beef Island; Sheet 4, Peter Island; Sheet 5, Virgin Gorda; Sheet 6, Anegada. These are all in colour and show political divisions, topographical, communication and other features. The maps are available from Ordinance Survey, Romsey Road, Southampton, England SO9 4DH and also from Survey Department, PO Box 142, Road Town, Tortola, British Virgin Islands.

44 **National Parks and Protected Areas map, British Virgin Islands.**
Road Town, Tortola: National Parks Trust, [n.d.].
This map shows the location of parks and protected areas throughout the islands. The name-index to locations also indicates the year when each was designated a national park. The scale is 1:26,400.

45 **The Tortola Plantation map.**
Rob Wilkinson. London: The author, 1798.
This important historical map which was drawn from the actual survey by George King for Isaac Pickering, a Quaker and estate owner, shows individual estates and their boundaries. A reference index guides the user to the names of owners and the use made of each estate at the time. The map, which was reprinted in 1985 by the Virgin Islands' Public Library and the Caribbean Printing Company, is available from the Public Library, Road Town, Tortola, British Virgin Islands.

## Virgin Islands, US

46 **Puerto Rico, Virgin Islands, St. Croix.**
Karto und Grafik. Frankfurt, Germany: Hildebrand Urlaubskarte, 1990. (Hildebrand Travel Maps, no. 53).
An excellent travel map (scale 1:294,000) with comprehensive tourist information and town plans. It includes individual maps of all the United States Virgin Islands, showing roads, distances, beaches, churches, airports, national parks and marine features.

47 **A St. Croix map of 1766.**
Walademar Westergaurd. *Journal of Negro History*, vol. 23, no. 2 (April 1938), p. 216-28.
The map shows the names and location of estates on St. Croix, United States Virgin Islands. There is also a note on the significance of St. Croix in a West Indian plantation economy.

48 **Map of St. Thomas, Danish West Indies.**
Amsterdam: MAPes MONDe Prints, *circa* 1684.
This late-17th-century map is the first known published map of St. Thomas. It shows houses and plantations of the early Danish colony in the West Indies. Fort Christian, the old Danish fort, is prominently featured.

# Sailing and cruising guides

## General

49 **Cruising guide to the Virgin Islands.**
Edited by Simon Scott, Nancy Scott. Charwater, Florida: Cruising Guide Publications, 1989. 242p. maps.
A complete illustrated guide to sailing, diving and fishing in the Virgin Islands. It contains sections such as: planning the cruise; cruising information; diving and snorkelling, anchorages; eating ashore; medical hints; and fishing in the waters.

50 **Southern chartering.**
Judith Watson. *Yachting*, vol. 156 (Aug. 1984), p. 64-70.
A comprehensive guide to bareboat fleets in the Virgin Islands, the Bahamas, Western Caribbean and Florida.

51   **Virgin Islands cruising guide.**
     Alexander C. Forbes.   [n.p.], Florida: Dukane, 1970. 119p.
This guide to routes and discoveries around the islands is well illustrated in colour and
is of relevance to both groups of islands. There is a useful index.

# Virgin Islands, UK and US

52   **Making the most of the British Virgin Islands.**
     Bill Robinson.   *Yachting*, vol. 159 (Jan. 1986), p. 49-51.
Robinson describes cruising conditions and anchoring spots in what he thinks 'is the
most popular of all chartering areas' in the region.

53   **Treasured islands.**
     Mag Lukena.   *Oceana*, vol. 21 (April 1988), p. 43-50.
The claim is made in this article that the beauty of the British Virgin Islands is as great
as when Columbus discovered them. A directory of where to go and what to do in the
islands is also included.

**Letters from the Virgin Islands.**
*See* item no. 116.

**Narrative of a visit to the West Indies.**
*See* item no. 117.

**A historical account of St. Thomas, West Indies.**
*See* item no. 129.

**In Danish times.**
*See* item no. 131.

**Tortola: a Quaker experiment of long ago in the tropics.**
*See* item no. 189.

# Travellers' Accounts

## Pre 20th century

54 **Familiar letters to Henry Clay of Kentucky describing a winter in the West Indies.**
J.J. Gurney. New York: Mahlon Day, 1840. 203p.
This account rather mocks the chilly winters of the Americas and seems intended to charm away its citizens to resettle in the islands.

55 **A voyage in the West Indies.**
John Augustine Waller. London: [n.p.], 1820. 106p.
Waller recounts his experience in the West Indies, paying much attention to scenic and geographical details and the weather situation. Tortola is described on pages 67-8.

56 **West India sketch book.**
London: Whitaker, 1834. (A reprint).
Records a miscellany of facts and figures which give economic and social insights into the state of the West Indies in the 17th and 18th centuries. Chapters 9-15 deal with Tortola.

# 20th century

**57 The turtle dove, the fat Virgin and the Saints.**
Harry Luke. In: *Caribbean Circuit.* London: Nicholson & Watson, 1950. 261p.
The British and United States Virgin Islands are both given fair treatment in this account (pages 151-69) of journeying in the Caribbean.

**58 Virgin Islands.**
George T. Eggleston. Princeton, New Jersey: D. van Nostrand, 1959. 208p. maps.
A facinating description of a month's cruise around the Virgin Islands on a fifty-foot ketch. There are close encounters on St. Thomas, St. John, Norman Island, Peter Island, Dead Man's Chest, Tortola, Beef Island, Guana Island, Marina Cay, Virgin Gorda, Anegada, Little Thatch, Jost Van Dyke and St. Croix. The pictures are large and impressive and record views of society in the 1950s.

## Virgin Islands, UK

**59 Lagooned in the British Virgin Islands.**
Hazel Ballance Eadie. London: George Routledge, 1931. 443p. map.
Eadie confesses to being curiously drawn to the magic of enchanting islands, and she manages to recapture some scenery, incidents and characters of the 1930s. Some West Indian proverbs and old-time sayings are included and these, along with eight plates and a chronology, make the imagery more real.

**60 You're welcome!**
Grahame Tharp. *Geographical Magazine*, vol. 31. no. 3. (July 1958), p. 149-58.
The author captures the friendliness of the islanders in this colourful article about personal encounters with them.

## Virgin Islands, US

**61 Crossroad of the buccaneers.**
Hendrik de Leeaw. London: Arco, 1957.
On pages 93-127 there is a descriptive account of the Virgin Islands of 'Uncle Sam', i.e. the United States Virgin Islands.

62 **Cruzan cruising: the forgotten virgin.**
Martin Luray, Jim McNitt. *Sail*, vol. 12. (Sept 1981), p. 85-91.
St. Croix is the forgotten Virgin in this item, but the author restores confidence in its charming scenery, beaches and commercial possibilities. The article is vibrantly illustrated.

63 **Lands of delight.**
Eleanor Early. Boston, Massachusetts: Houghton, 1939. 214p.
This cruise to northern South America and the Caribbean took in Sir Francis Drake's Channel and the British Virgin Islands. The journey through the renowned water highway and its numerous islands is delightfully described.

64 **These are the Virgin Islands.**
Hamilton Cochran. New York: Prentice Hall, 1937. 236p.
The work concentrates on the three largest islands of the United States Virgin Islands – St. Croix, St. Thomas and St. John.

65 **Virgin Islands.**
Fritz Henle. New York: Hastings House, 1922. 72p.
This is a traveller's account of the Virgin Islands in pictures, with text by V.T. Winterry. It illustrates the dynamic natural beauty of the islands with scenes of market life, folk-life and architecture.

66 **Virgin Islands: tropical playland of the United States of America.**
John Scofield. *National Geographic Magazine*, vol. 109, no. 2 (Feb. 1956). maps.
The article illustrates life on the island of St. Thomas in the 1950s, highlighting the town of Charlotte Amalie, the Old Fort Christian, carnival, and vegetable growing.

# Tourism

## Guides and information

### Virgin Islands, UK

67  **Discover nature's little secrets.**
New York: British Virgin Islands Tourist Board. 1991. 14p. map.
'Nature's little secrets have always held the key to a special way of life in the British Virgin Islands' is the quotation which introduces this gallery of irresistible sights of the country, the people, hideaway clubs and villas. Luxury resorts, secret treasures and crimson sunsets all conspire to enhance the natural surroundings. It is a tastefully designed little publication, which should arouse curiosity about the islands in all who read it.

68  **Virgin Islands travel guide.**
Staff of Editions Berlitz.   Lausanne, Switzerland: Berlitz, 1977. 128p.
maps.
A compact and colourful guide, giving quick facts and clear-cut answers to tourist questions, from the location of the telegram office to the cost of a particular guided tour. The guide is well researched with exciting historical details and tours around the islands. The book is distributed by Macmillan in New York and by Cassell in London.

69  **British Virgin Islands tourist handbook, 1990.**
Edited by Vernon Pickering, illustrated by Jon Osman, Jonathan
Peter.   Road Town, Tortola: Laurel Publications International, 1990.
123p. maps.

Each issue carries useful up-to-date tourist information but there are also substantial articles on such topics as old coins, stamps, historic monuments and national parks. It has appeared annually since 1985, with Giorgio Migliavacca as associate editor. The maps in this issue were drawn by Jon Osman and the island sketches by Jonathan Peter.

70  **Welcome to our British Virgin Islands.**
Claudia Colli, illustrated by Norma Wells, foreword by Chief Minister,
Lavity Stoutt.   Road Town, Tortola: British Virgin Islands Tourist
Board, 1983. 36p. map. bibliog.

A cultural and historical tour designed as an introduction to many aspects of life in the islands. There are chapters on geography, history, historic sites, flora and fauna, national parks and other points of interest. The booklet was designed and charmingly illustrated by Norma Wells.

**The Caribbean, Bermuda and the Bahamas 1991.**
*See* item no. 1.

**Discover.**
*See* item no. 10.

**Treasure islands: a guide to the British Virgin Islands.**
*See* item no. 13.

**Study of mini-cruise ships: British Virgin Islands.**
*See* item no. 323.

**The welcome: tourist guide.**
*See* item no. 562.

# Virgin Islands, US

71  **St. John on foot and by car.**
Randall S. Koladis, illustrated by Thomas B. Howell.   Washington,
DC: West Indies Publishing Company, 1976. 53p. maps.

One in a beautifully produced series, this is an excellent walking and motoring guide to the history and charm of St. John, the most virgin of the United States Virgin Islands. In addition to a brief history, it contains three self-guided tours of the island: a walking and motoring tour of the north side of St. John, an exploratory trip along Centerline Road and a hike down the Reef Bay Trail. The attractive illustrations of island scenes were done by Thomas B. Howell.

72  **St. Thomas on foot and by car.**
Randall S. Koladis, illustrated by Thomas B. Howell.   Washington,
DC: West Indies Publishing Company, 1976. 55p. maps.
This guide offers visitors proverbs, history, trails and tours of St. Thomas. It contains a
walking tour of Charlotte Amalie and a motoring guide to historic sites and points of
interest scattered throughout the island.

73  **Visitors guide: Virgin Islands playground.**
Edited by Frances E. Newbold.   Charlotte Amalie, St. Thomas: Island
Media, 1990. map.
This is a handy and comprehensive guide to St. Thomas, incorporating history, tours,
and directories to restaurants, shops, transportation, customs and other tourist
information.

74  **Where: Virgin Islands.**
Nancy Davis.   Charlotte Amalie, St. Thomas: Newhart and Associates,
1990. 32p.
This guide to St. Thomas covers many different features of the island. It includes
directories to real estate, beaches, points of interest, night-life, where to shop, and
water sports.

# Social and economic impact

75  **Regional tourism: economic planning, policy and research workshop.**
Christ Church, Barbados: Caribbean Tourism Research Centre, 1988.
46p.
The report of a conference held on 9-11 December 1987. It covers some of the
important topics affecting the tourist trade in the region: economic policy, economic
research, economic development, tourism policy, tourism development, input–output
analysis, data retrieval and economic systems.

76  **Report of the seminar on Tourism Management and Environmental
Issues.**
Road Town, Tortola: British Virgin Islands Tourist Board, 1988. 142p.
This report contains the conclusions arrived at by participants attending the seminar
from ten Caribbean countries, including the British Virgin Islands. Topics discussed
include pollution of coastal areas; building rules and regulations covering areas
designated for development of hotels and villas; and local enforcement of international
regulations listed by the World Tourism Organization. The seminar was held on 14-15
October 1988.

**Tourism.** Social and economic impact

77 **Tourism and perspectives of cultural change on Virgin Gorda: patterns and processes.**
James W. Lett, Jr.   Master's thesis, University of Florida, 1980. 70p.
Lett's work traces the development of tourism in the British Virgin Islands. It considers tourist and native perspectives on tourism on Virgin Gorda; examines the differences in expectations; and confirms several patterns of cultural change in the islands.

78 **Tourism in Tortola, British Virgin Islands: perceptions towards land carrying capacity.**
Christopher D.B. Howell.   Master's thesis, University of Florida, 1978. 281p. maps. bibliog.
This thesis examines the impact of tourism on the islands. The author concludes that it is important for the Government to formulate a comprehensive policy, emphasizing which additional tourist facilities should be permitted and where. They ought also to determine the overall limits to growth.

79 **Tourism management, environmental and developmental issues.**
British Virgin Islands Tourist Board.   Road Town, Tortola: Chief Minister's Office, 1987. 90p.
The papers and the summary report of a seminar held in Tortola on 14-15 October 1987. Papers presented are: 1. 'Tourism management: public sector issues' by Elton Georges; 2. 'Environmental education in schools' by Nicholas Clark; 3. 'Tourism and environmental education in schools' by Louis Potter; 4. 'Approaches to successful tourism development, environmental protection and management in the British Virgin Islands' by Eric Blommestein and Luther Gorgon Miller; 5. 'Land and land policies: implications for tourism and the environment' by Lorna Smith; 6. 'Tourism in the British Virgin Islands: economic performance and development objectives' by Pierre Encontre.

80 **Why does the tourist dollar matter?: an introduction to the economics of tourism in the British Virgin Islands.**
Pierre Encontre.   Road Town, Tortola: British Virgin Islands Tourist Board, 1989. 141p. maps. bibliog.
This study reveals facts and mechanisms which a vibrant community should lean on in order to fulfil its development objectives. It suggests that the tourist trade is important to the British Virgin Islands, not only through its present economic impact, but also because an increased local input to the tourism product can enhance the standard of living of the community. Some aspects covered are: raising the standard of living of an island community; tourism income multiplier; existing benefits from tourism; and tourism and wealth in the British Virgin Islands. Several pictures and graphs illustrate the text, and there is also a useful glossary.

# Flora and Fauna

## Flora

### General

81  **Cactus studies in the West Indies.**
N.L. Britton.  *Journal of the New York Botanical Garden*, vol. 14,
no. 161 (1913), p. 99.
In this general article on cactus species of the region, there are several references to
species found on Tortola, and mention is also made of the primeval forest found on
Sage Mountain.

82  **Caribbean flora.**
C.D. Adams.  [n.p.], Surrey, England: Thomas Nelson, 1976. 63p.
A study of selected Caribbean flowers and plants giving their classification, structure,
physiology and economic importance. Lavishly illustrated, it is useful for comparison
with other standard works.

83  **Common trees of Puerto Rico and the Virgin Islands.**
Elbert Little.  Washington, DC: Department of Agriculture, 1964.
548p.
This guide gives the scientific and common names, origin and current island habitat of
trees. Large-scale drawings and illustrations accompany the descriptions, making it a
very good study text.

84 **Flora and fauna of the Caribbean.**
Peter R. Bacon.   Port of Spain, Trinidad: Key Caribbean Publications, 1978. 319p. maps.

A general introduction to the ecology of the Caribbean area which takes the form of an ecological tour – from Caribbean rainforest to coral reefs, sand beaches and rocky shores; mangrove swamps; rivers; savannas; caves; desert islands; and man-made environments. There are over 200 line drawings and photographs, plus 32 full-colour plates. Although only St. Croix of the Virgin Islands group is mentioned, the general background and ecological principles apply to the entire area. The work is aimed at naturalists and students but will also interest anyone who wishes to understand the relationships of life in the natural environment.

# Virgin Islands, UK and US

85 **Scientific survey of Puerto Rico and the Virgin Islands.**
New York: New York Academy of Sciences, 1927. 24 vols.

The Academy deals with the description of flora, mosses, insects, marine animals. Several of the volumes examine the characteristics of species found in both groups of Virgin Islands.

86 **Trees for urban use in Puerto Rico and the Virgin Islands.**
Thomas H. Schubert.   Rio Piedras, Puerto Rico: Institute of Tropical Forestry in cooperation with the University of Puerto Rico, 1979. 91p.

An indispensable guide to useful trees for shade and ornament in Puerto Rico and the Virgin Islands. Forty-six species of trees are described and illustrated. Information is also provided about planting, maintenance and appropriate use in urban areas.

87 **Tropical blossoms.**
Dorothy Hargreaves, Bob Hargreaves.   [n.p.], Oregon: Hargreaves Industrial, [n.d.]. 48p.

The authors have produced a handy guide to the botany of selected flowering plants of the Virgin Islands. Some of the illustrations are page-size photographs in full colour and these could even stimulate an interest in photography.

88 **Trees of Jost Van Dyke.**
Elbert L. Little.   Rio Piedras, Puerto Rico: Institute of Tropical Forestry, 1969. 12p.

Sixty-nine tree specimens are recorded here as native to Jost Van Dyke, British Virgin Islands, and eighteen others are noted as having been introduced. The work is based on field studies and it provides distribution records of species previously known from adjacent islands.

89    **Poisonous and injurious plants of the United States Virgin Islands.**
A.J. Oates, James O. Butcher.    [n.p.]: Cooperative Extension Service,
1981. 3rd ed. 97p.
Characterized by its descriptive details, the work is indexed by both the scientific name
and the common name of each plant it identifies. Forty-eight illustrations further
enhance the usefulness of this book which is now in its third printing. It was first
published in 1962.

# Fauna

## General

90    **Birds of the West Indies.**
James Bond.    Boston, Massachusetts: Houghton Mifflin, 1961. 256p.
Bond's classic guide to Caribbean birds gives classification, characteristics and habitats
of birds in the region. Several references are made to Virgin Islands locations.

91    **Butterflies and other insects of the Eastern Caribbean.**
P.D. Stiling.    London: Macmillan, 1986. 85p.
A beginner's guide to the entomology of the region, with clear and bold illustrations.

## Virgin Islands, UK

92    **Annotated check list of the birds, mammals, reptiles and amphibians of
the Virgin Islands and Puerto Rico.**
Richard Philibosian, John A. Yntema.    Frederiksted, St. Croix:
Informational Services, 1977. 48p.
This checklist includes individual entries for 393 living and extinct species. Local
occurrence is given for seven geographical areas including St. Thomas and its cays, St.
John and its cays, the British Virgin Islands, Anegada, St. Croix and its cays.
Notations are given to identify those species that are endemic, endangered, extinct,
breeding locally, introduced, and accidental. The seasons of local occurrence are also
indicated. Both authors have studied the flora and fauna of the Virgin Islands for many
years.

## Birds

93  **Birds of the Virgin Islands.**
Dea Murray.  St. Thomas: The author, 1969. 28p.
A simple identification guide to the birds of the composite group of islands. Each entry has a drawing (in colour) of the male bird, while the female, if different in colouring, is described in the text. Local and scientific names, size, nesting habits, number of eggs laid and the sound of voice are detailed. An additional list of rare immigrants and birds not reported in sufficient areas to warrant full description, is appended. The guide is based on authentic observations of bird watchers located in various parts of three major islands.

94  **Birds list of the British Virgin Islands.**
B.P. Holloway.  Road Town, Tortola: National Parks Trust, [n.d.]. 8p. map.
Very well produced, the list gives the scientific and common names; status – whether resident or permanent; the seasons they appear; and relative abundance – whether rare, uncommon, common or hypothetical. A useful list of sources is also given.

95  **Cambridge ornithological expedition to the British Virgin Islands.**
Cambridge, England: Churchill College, 1977. 44p. maps. bibliog.
This report of the 1976 expedition is a brief but intense study of the birds – species, characteristics and habitats – found throughout the islands. There are habitat maps, a table of islands and species, and a biogeographical report.

## Reptiles

96  **Reptiles and amphibians of the Virgin Islands.**
Witham P. Maclean, illustrated by Karen Bertrand.  London: Macmillan Education, 1982. 54p. map.
This study lists and describes species of reptiles and amphibians which are native to the islands. Dr Maclean also provides selected references and a well-compiled index.

## Marine animals

97  **Sea turtles of the British Virgin Islands.**
Karen L. Eckert.  Road Town, Tortola: Conservation Office, Ministry of Natural Resources and Labour, [n.d., but possibly 1990]. 8p.
Designed to enhance a public education programme aimed at greater concern for endangered species, this publication very simply describes the characteristics of the sea turtle, the species and habitats. It also tells why sea turtles are endangered and reproduces the section of the law which makes it illegal to catch, slaughter, buy or sell the animal or its eggs. It is brilliantly prepared by the Wider Caribbean Sea Turtle Conservation Network (WIDECAST), in association with the British Virgin Islands National Parks Trust and the Conservation and Fisheries Department. The text and

design are both by Dr Eckert and funding was provided by the United States Fish and Wildlife Service and the Chelonia Institute. Teachers and youth groups would welcome this little informative publication for their 'nature resource packs'.

### 98 Anegada: marine biological survey.
Richard Dunne, Barbara E. Brown.  Cambridge, England: Cambridge University Press, 1975. 63p.

A team of Cambridge scientists set out on an expedition to explore the marine biological nature of the territory's northernmost and flattest island. There are several illustrations and tables and a sizeable portion of the work is devoted to observations of the reef systems. Thirty species of coral are recorded on Anegada and comparisons are made with species on Cuba, Puerto Rico, Jamaica, and Bonaire.

## Butterflies

### 99 The butterflies of Anegada, British Virgin Islands, with descriptions of a new *Calisto* (Satyridae) and a new *Copaeodes* (Hesperiidae) endemic to the island.
David Spencer Smith, Lee D. Miller and Faustino McKensie.  *Bulletin of the Allyn Museum*, no. 133 (14 June 1991), p. 1-25. map. bibliog.

Professors Smith, Lee and McKensie announce to the scientific community the discovery on Anegada of the 'Calisto anegadensis' and the 'Copaeodes eoa', two new species of butterflies endemic to the island. The new species are painstakingly described and there are detailed illustrations showing the markings. The paper also describes twenty-two additional species of butterflies living on Anegada. The study was carried out over a period of five years, commencing in 1986. One of the scientists, Professor Smith of the Hope Entomological Collections at University Museum, Oxford, England, said that the discovery 'adds entomology to the fascination of Anegada'. (The paper is dedicated to the memory of John Griffith of Jesus College, Oxford, and is published as a separate document by the Florida Museum of Natural History, University of Florida, Gainesville, Florida.)

**Treasure islands: a guide to the British Virgin Islands.**
*See* item no. 13.

**Welcome to our British Virgin Islands.**
*See* item no. 70.

**Agricultural Exhibition, Industry and Nutrition Week: develop the British Virgin Islands wealth through agriculture, industry and health.**
*See* item no. 343.

**Livestock development.**
*See* item no. 349.

**Report of the Department of Agriculture.**
*See* item no. 350.

**The Botanic Garden: a project.**
*See* item no. 410.

# Virgin Islands, US

100 **Guide to corals and fishes of Florida, the Bahamas and the Caribbean.**
Idaz Greenberg. Miami, Florida: Seahawk Press, 1977. 64p.

A general handy reference to 260 species of corals and fishes, illustrated in full colour. It gives the local and scientific names of the species, their chief characteristics and their length. An index further enhances the volume's usefulness.

101 **Survey of leatherback turtle nesting sites.**
G. Cambers, H. Lima. Road Town, Tortola: Conservation Office, 1989. maps.

The leatherback turtle has long been a recognizable part of the culture of the Virgin Islands but is fast becoming an endangered species. This survey of nesting sites in the territory provides a base whereby some measure of protection would be drafted and enforced.

102 **The living reef: corals and fishes of Florida, the Bahamas, Bermuda and the Caribbean.**
Idaz Greenberg. [n.p.], USA: Graphic Sales Innovators, 1974. 111p.

The guide is lavishly illustrated with large photographs in full colour. The formation of coral reefs is explained and an index to both the common and the scientific names of corals and fishes make this book popular with young marine enthusiasts.

**Afro-Caribbean folk medicine.**
*See* item no. 212.

**Edible fruits and vegetables of the English-speaking Caribbean.**
*See* item no. 347.

**Agriculture and food fair of the Virgin Islands.**
*See* item no. 351.

**Avocado production and marketing.**
*See* item no. 352.

**Gardeners' factsheet.**
*See* item no. 354.

**Sorrel production and marketing in the United States Virgin Islands.**
*See* item no. 355.

# Prehistory and Archaeology

## General

### 103   On the trail of the Arawaks.
Fred Olsen, foreword by George Kubler, introductory essay by Irving Rousse.   Norman, Oklahoma: University of Oklahoma Press, 1974. 408p. maps. bibliog.

The author reveals the story of his search for the origins of the first Indians encountered by Christopher Columbus on his voyages to the New World. He explains how his team discovered the Arawaks; he expounds their religion, petroglyphs, culture and games. He traces their origins from Saladero to the Antilles as evidenced in an eight-page section of colour photos describing Arawak sites and sculpture. There are also many illustrations showing shards, bowls, tools, zemis and petroglyphs found throughout the Lesser Antilles, but especially in Antigua. Pottery from St. Croix is shown on pages 228 and 364-5, and on page 213 there is a typical Indian ball court that Gudmund Hatt found at Salt River on St. Croix. Reference is also made to the fragment of a ball court belt found by Dick Richards not far from Salt River in the 1950s. This is an important work on the archaeology of the entire region and has already had significant bearing on establishing the authenticity of later finds in other islands in the Virgin group.

### 104   Papers in Caribbean anthropolopy.
Edited by Irving Rousse, compiled by Sidney Mitz.   Yale, New Haven: Department of Anthropology, Yale University, 1960. bibliog. (Yale University Publications in Anthropology, nos 57-64).

Eight papers which deal with some sociological, economic, archaeological and ethnological problems of the Caribbean. The article by Rousse, entitled 'The entry of man into the West Indies', questions how and from where the aboriginal *Homo caribensis* arrived in the islands. It makes for stimulating reading.

# Virgin Islands, UK

**105 The British Virgin Islands archaeological survey: first season.**
Afredo E. Figueredo. *Indian Notes*, vol. 8. no. 4 (Fall 1972).
(Published in New York by the Museum of the American Indian, Heye
Foundation, 1972).

Based on the finds of an archaeological survey team, this report reveals much evidence
of Arawakan culture on the island of Virgin Gorda, British Virgin Islands. The
expedition, which is described in great detail, was sponsored by the Museum of the
American Indian in cooperation with the British Virgin Islands government and is the
first professional archaeological survey ever conducted in the islands. There are
illustrations of a decorated Indian spindle whorl, the most complete to be found in the
region. In addition, reference is made to the unearthing of several mounds of
prehistoric artefacts and concentrations of aboriginal pottery which had lain
undisturbed for centuries.

**106 Pre-history of the Virgin Islands – part one.**
Jill Tattersall. *BVI Beacon*, vol. 6, no. 1 (8 June 1989), p. 38.

Using some of the author's original research on the prehistory of the Virgin Islands,
this article takes one back to 10,000 years ago when Puerto Rico and the Virgin
Islands, excluding St. Croix, were still one island and animals such as giant armadillos,
sloths, anteaters, porcupines, monkeys, crocodiles and alligators, rabbits, squirrels and
capybara abounded. It describes the first inhabitants as the small Mongoloid archaic
peoples who were descendants of the South American hunters. The author has
presented her research to assemblies such as the Americanists and the International
Association for Caribbean Archaeology.

**The West Indian Islands.**
*See* item no. 7.

**From Columbus to Castro: the history of the Caribbean 1492-1969.**
*See* item no. 111.

**A concise history of the British Virgin Islands.**
*See* item no. 120.

**A history of the British Virgin Islands, 1672 to 1970.**
*See* item no. 122.

# Virgin Islands, US

**107 Sculptured stones of St. Thomas.**
Katheryne Kay. *Virgin Islands Archaeological Society Journal*, vol. 1,
no. 3 (1976), [n.p.].

An illuminating account of the shapes, designs and functions of stones in early Virgin
Islands culture.

108   **The Virgin Islands as a historical frontier between the Tainos and the Caribs.**
Alfred E. Figueredo.    Frederiksted, St. Croix: 1979. 12p.
This is a study of both cultures and the influences each had on the islands in pre-columbian times.

109   **Virgin Islands prehistory.**
St. Croix: Aye Aye Press, 1974. 22p.
An objection is raised in this publication concerning the current development of prehistory, its expense, emphasis, and relevance to everyday life in the United States Virgin Islands.

**Foundation News.**
*See* item no. 579.

**Virgin Islands Archaeological Society Journal.**
*See* item no. 589.

# History

## General

**110  Caribbeana.**
V.L. Oliver.   London: [n.p.], 1910-19. 6 vols.
A collection of miscellaneous papers relating to the history, genealogy, topography and antiquities of the British West Indies. Volume three, which was published in 1914, contains references to Tortola and gives the pedigrees of the Lettsome, Hodge, Purcell and Georges families, all of which are common names in the British Virgin Islands.

**111  From Columbus to Castro: the history of the Caribbean 1492-1969.**
Eric Williams.   London: André Deutsch, 1970. 576p. maps. bibliog.
A general history of the region, dealing with all aspects of Caribbean history. On page 190, Williams attributes the two attempts to recognize the economic rights of negroes in the 18th century to the Quakers of Tortola. There are also four pages of details about the United States Virgin Islands.

**112  The growth of the modern West Indies.**
Gordon K. Lewis.   New York: Monthly Review Press, 1968. 506p.
A brilliant analysis and interpretation of modern West Indian society. It is comprehensive in scope and scholarly in treatment, analysing in detail the character of the various elements that have made up the whole of West Indian society. The British and United States Virgin Islands are mentioned on pages 337-42 in the chapter entitled: 'The problem of size: the Lesser groups'.

113 **History of the British West Indies.**
Alan Burns. London: Allen & Unwin, 1954. 2nd rev. ed., 1965. 849p.
maps. bibliog.
A comprehensive account of the history of the West Indies, including also detailed
descriptions of countries outside the 'British Empire'. The Virgin Islands are treated
comparatively, especially with regard to the part they played in supporting the
plantation economy and the maritime defence of international warfare.

# Virgin Islands, UK

114 **Historical account of the Virgin Islands in the West Indies.**
George Suckling. London: Benjamin White, 1780.
An account of the islands 'from their being settled by the English near a century ago to
their obtaining a Legislature of their own in 1773'. It also includes some legal
difficulties of the writer, who was also Chief Justice on the island of Tortola.

115 **The history, civil and commercial of the British colonies in the West
Indies.**
Bryan Edwards. London: John Stockdale, 1801. 3 vols.
The historical background of the British empire in the Caribbean. The relevance of the
British Virgin Islands to the realm is referred to in volume one, page 500. Several
other editions of the original work have been published in 1793, 1798, 1807, and 1966.

116 **Letters from the Virgin Islands.**
London: John Van Voorst, 1843. 243p. map.
The (anonymous) writer illustrates the life and manners in the West Indies and gives a
lively account of Virgin Island life in bygone days. References to the British Virgin
Islands are to be found on pages 50, 54, 166, 227-31, and include an interesting account
of the Nottingham estate at Long Look, Tortola, British Virgin Islands.

117 **Narrative of a visit to the West Indies in 1840 and 1841.**
George Truman, John Jackson, Thomas Longstreth. Philadelphia,
Pennsylvania: Merrihew and Thompson, 1844.
The narrative contains an account of a visit to Tortola, British Virgin Islands, with two
interesting illustrations showing the foundations of the Quakers' meeting-house at Fat
Hogs Bay, Tortola.

118 **The Virgin Islands, British West Indies.**
W.C. Fishlock. London: Waterlow, 1912. 30p.
An accurate handbook of information describing the general state of the islands almost
a century ago. The development of agricultural policies is emphasized and the ability of
one man to administer the hospital and control the government of the British islands, is
highlighted.

119  **The British Virgin Islands: a chronology.**
Norwell Harrigan, Pearl Varlack.   Road Town, Tortola: Tortola
Research and Consulting Services, 1970. 33p. map. bibliog.
This useful booklet highlights British Virgin Islands history from 1493 to 1969. The
dates and their significance are clearly set out, providing a ready reference and
introduction to the islands' past.

120  **A concise history of the British Virgin Islands.**
Vernon W. Pickering.   New York; Milan, Italy: Falcon, 1987. 159p.
bibliog.
The work covers the Amerindians to 1986. Part One includes brief accounts of the first
inhabitants, the plantation period, slavery, missionaries, emancipation, agricultural
experimentation, political and social progress, development and cultural identity. Part
Two contains brief histories of Virgin Gorda, Anegada and Peter Islands and also
biographies of some famous Virgin Islanders: John Coackley Lettsome, John
Pickering, William Thornton, Richard Humphreys, Frederick Augustus Pickering,
Christopher Fleming, and Sir Olva Georges. Old and new drawings and photographs
admirably illustrate the text. The book was written with 'young students' in mind and
the glossary illustrates this; the bibliography and index also serve well.

121  **Early history of the British Virgin Islands: from Columbus to
emancipation.**
Vernon Pickering.   [n.p.]: Falcon, 1983. 248p. bibliog. maps.
An historical overview covering legends of saints and pirates; trade; law and order;
missionaries and religion; slavery and emancipation; famous Virgin Islanders;
communications and postal history of the British Virgin Islands. Several historical
maps and other illustrations – for example 'A bay in Tortola 140 years ago' on page 89
– enhance the value of this book. Long passages from original sources are also quoted
out of respect for the 'credible image of the historical reality', which those documents
faithfully convey.

122  **A history of the British Virgin Islands, 1672 to 1970.**
Isaac Dookhan.   Epping, England: Caribbean University Press in
association with Bowker, 1975. 255p. maps. bibliog.
A detailed history which covers the right of sovereignty, slavery and emancipation,
social services and 20th-century considerations. It is one of two substantial works
published about the islands in the same year.

123  **Lettsom: his life, times, friends and descendants.**
James Johnston Abraham.   London: William Heinemann Medical
Books, 1933. 498p.
An enlightened account of Lettsome, a medical doctor of international repute, who
was born on Jost Van Dyke, British Virgin Islands. It is well illustrated and indexed.

124 **The public market: a historic scene.**
Janice Nibbs. *Virgin Islands Historical Documents*, vol. 1. no. 3
(Aug.-Sept. 1984), p. 6-7.

A glance backwards to the years before 1953 when 'everything that was not exported
to the United States Virgin Islands was transported to town by donkeys, mules and on
heads'. The article traces the development of the market place in various locations: in
front of the Administration building; Chalwell Street; and on Wickham's Cay opposite
Esso Station. Two illustrations accompany the article: one of the market place in 1912
and the other of it in 1958.

125 **Tales of Tortola and the British Virgin Islands.**
Florence Lewisohn. [n.p.]: [n.p.], 1986. 89p. map. bibliog.

First published in 1976, this is a revised sixth printing of a chatty but informative work.
It is an interesting account of nearly five centuries of lore, legend, and general history
of the islands including incidental information on specific islands. It is a good, brief
introductory history generously illustrated with old prints, and based both on primary
and secondary sources. The last chapter is a mini-encyclopaedia of some of the larger
islands which have had their moments of wealth, glory and fame in the European era.
It is extremely popular and is available from Island Services, Road Town, Tortola,
British Virgin Islands. The author has also written several books on the United States
Virgin Islands.

126 **The Virgin Islands story.**
Norwell Harrigan, Pearl Varlack. Epping, England: Caribbean
University Press and Bowker, 1975. 213p. maps. bibliog.

This is a facinating study which brings together the past and present history of the
British Virgin Islands, within the framework of a comprehensive analysis. The authors,
both eminent historians, combined their experience as teachers and administrators,
and their insights gained from belonging to the islands, to produce a classic work. It is
well illustrated and indexed and also has useful appendixes. Both authors, British
Virgin Islanders, were professors at the College of the Virgin Islands in the United
States Virgin Islands. The late Dr Harrigan held the directorship of the Caribbean
Research Institute for several years.

**British Virgin Islands: territorial report for the year 1987.**
*See* item no. 9.

**The Virgins: a descriptive and historical profile.**
*See* item no. 25.

Maps and atlases, various.
*See* items 41-8.

**The Tortola Plantation map.**
*See* item no. 45.

**Caribbean Quakers.**
*See* item no. 181.

**Methodism: two hundred years in the British Virgin Islands.**
*See* item no. 188.

Tortola: a Quaker experiment of long ago in the tropics.
*See* item no. 189.

The growth of the operation of the judicial system of the British Virgin Islands.
*See* item no. 265.

Report of the British Virgin Islands constitutional conference.
*See* item no. 266.

Chief monuments of the British Virgin Islands.
*See* item no. 400.

An inventory of shipwrecks of the Virgin Islands, 1523-1825.
*See* item no. 403.

Four flakes of dust: a study of the Long Bay cannon.
*See* item no. 404.


# Virgin Islands, US

127 **Brief history of the Virgin Islands.**
J. Antonio Jarvis.   St. Thomas: The Art Shop, 1938. 258p. map.
Charming drawings of social life and photographs of official meetings enliven this brief and elegantly written history. It grew out of the vision of the author, a high-school Social Studies teacher, and his faith in the local community. This important social and historical work by a native Virgin Islander covers the discovery, settlement, slavery, American interests and the 1936 Organic Act of the islands.

128 **Divers information on the romantic history of St. Croix: from the time of Columbus until today.**
Florence Lewisohn.   Christiansted, St Croix: St. Croix Landmarks Society, 1964. 69p. bibliog.
This small but popular booklet about the island was published for the benefit of the St. Croix Landmarks Society's restoration and preservation projects. It offers brief accounts of: the age of opulence, sugarcane plantations, St. Croix sugar mills, rum and revolutions, the century of change, folklore, and historic sites.

129 **A historical account of St. Thomas, West Indies.**
John P. Knox.   New York: Charles Scribner, 1852. 271p. maps.
A crisp record of progress in commerce, missions and churches; climate and adaptation. There are also lucid descriptions of the geological structure; natural history; botany; slave insurrections; emancipation and condition of the labouring classes in the 18th century.

130 **A history of the Virgin Islands of the United States.**
Isaac Dookhan. Epping, England: Caribbean University Press and
Bowker, 1974. 321p. maps. bibliog.
This is an important comprehensive history of the United States Virgin Islands. It
covers four centuries and tells of successive waves of European immmigrants; slavery
and exploitation punctuated by uprisings; missionaries and colonial change; trade
decline and an upsurge in tourism. Well researched and documented with references at
the end of each chapter, the work is narrated and interpreted with the diligence and
expertise of an eminent scholar who received his doctorate from the University of the
West Indies. Dookhan, at the time of publication, was Associate Professor of History
and historian writer-in-residence of the College of the Virgin Islands, United States
Virgin Islands.

131 **In Danish times.**
Lucie Horlyk, translated by Betty Nilson. Stockholm: Barnangen,
1969. 84p.
These are stories about life in St. Croix and St. Thomas during the first half of the
century. Edit Lenden designed the cover but other illustrations are by Panohita
Canfield. The book is part of a collection called 'Under the tropical sun', first
published in 1913.

132 **St. Croix at the 20th century: a chapter in its history.**
D.C. Canegata. New York: Carlton, 1968. 161p.
An authentic account which deals with events up to the introduction of the 1906
Colonial Law or Organic Act. There are also the following useful appendixes: St.
Thomas and dependencies; Land divisions; and List of properties destroyed during the
riot of 1878.

133 **St. Croix under seven flags.**
Florence Lewisohn. [n.p.], Florida: Dukane, 1970. 432p.
Lewisohn reflects on five centuries of turbulence and sweeping changes in this
Caribbean island. St. Croix has flown the flags of Spain, England, Holland, Denmark
and the United States of America. The whole spectrum of history, from Columbus's
fight with the Caribs at Salt River Bay to 20th-century mixed blessings caused by a fast-
expanding economy, is drawn in this historical cavalcade of one island. It is lavishly
illustrated with old reproductions ranging from the late 1400s to the present day.

134 **St. John backtime.**
Ruth Hull Low, Raphael Valls. St. John: Eden Hill, 1985. 94p. maps.
bibliog.
A rich source of eye-witness accounts from 1718 to 1956, narrating two and a half
centuries of life on St. John, one of the islands which was once part of the Danish West
Indies. The work is a treasury of contemporary maps, plans, drawings, paintings and
photographs from archives, libraries, museums and private collections in the Virgin
Islands and America, Canada, Norway and Denmark.

135  **Trials and triumphs: the big road to a middle class society in the United States Virgin Islands.**
Earle Ottley.   Charlotte Amalie, St. Thomas: The author, 1982. 488p.
A very important report on the effort of Virgin Islanders to move from grinding poverty to relative prosperity and political maturity. It covers the period from 1940 to the 1970s – an important and exciting era of Virgin Islands history. There is a selection of illustrations of the men and women who shaped the islands' destiny. The author also discusses development, migration and politics in a pre-industrial society.

136  **The United States Virgin Islands.**
Luther Zabriskie.   Stovington, Maine: George F. Bush; Mainespring, 1985. 167p.
An indispensable source for the early history of each island. It records historical and descriptive accounts, commercial and industrial facts, figures and resources. Chapter 9 describes the West India Company and other companies; Chapter 22 outlines education and religion; Chapter 24 describes the hurricane of 1916 and Chapter 26 records the formal transfer of the islands. There are twenty pages of illustrations – a treasure trove for the researcher. This edition is, however, abridged from the original which was first published in 1918.

137  **Conquest of Eden.**
Michael Paiewonsky.   Rome: MAPes MONDe, 1990. 176p. maps.
This skilfully written book is an historical work set during the second, third and fourth voyages of Christopher Columbus through the Virgin Islands, Puerto Rico and Hispaniola. It is complemented by sixty-one illustrations, some of which are in colour. Quotes from the ship's journal of Columbus often accompany the illustrations and in these, canny humour may sometimes be found. Some of the illustrations are of great historical value; for instance, a drawing from 1529 depicting two Indians playing a ball game; and a 1904 photograph depicting the St. John petroglyphs. This is an outstanding addition to Caribbean/Virgin Islands history records. (Available from MAPes MONDe Ltd, P. Montevecchio, 6, 00186 Rome, Italy and from: PO Box 6545, St. Thomas, United States Virgin Islands, 00804).

**People of passion.**
*See* item no. 14.

**Profiles of outstanding Virgin Islanders, vol. 2.**
*See* item no. 15.

**Virgin Islands picture book.**
*See* item no. 17.

Maps and atlases, various.
*See* items 46-8.

**Virgin Islands.**
*See* item no. 65.

**Historic churches of the Virgin Islands.**
*See* item no. 191.

**The history of the African Methodist Episcopal Church in the Virgin Islands.**
*See* item no. 192.

**Praise God: two hundred years 1773-1973, history of the Catholic Church of St. Thomas.**
*See* item no. 193.

**Religious development.**
*See* item no. 195.

**The Virgin Islands story: history of the Lutheran State Church and other churches . . .**
*See* item no. 196.

# Slavery and emancipation

## Virgin Islands, UK

138 **The slavery of the British West India Islands.**
James Stephen.  London: J. Butterworth & Son, 1824. 2 vols.
Reprinted, New York: Kraus, 1969.
Two volumes in one: volume one deals with the laws relating to slavery in the islands and volume two looks at the actual practice of slavery, that is, the management, treatment of slaves, etc.

139 **The Abolition Act 1833.**
Edited by V.P. Moll.  Road Town, Tortola: Virgin Islands Public
Library in association with the Central Committee for the Observation
of 150 Years of Human Advancement. 44p. Reprinted 1984.
The intention of this reprint, in the words of the editor, is 'to evoke some thought on what the Abolition Act meant to our forefathers and what it should be saying to us today'. It is prefaced with a number of important articles written by local historians and legislators: Governor David R. Barwick; Speaker Keith Flax; Honourable Cyril B. Romney; Honourable Willard Wheatley; Honourable H.L. Stoutt; lawyer McWelling Todman and Dr Norwell Harrigan.

140 **Causes for emancipation.**
Ermin Burnett.  *Virgin Islands Historical Documents*, vol. 1, no. 2
(May-June 1984), p. 2-4.
The writer describes the Act for the Abolition of Slavery as 'a major piece of human rights legislation passed in the British Caribbean' but also shows that 'economic forces and the insubordination by slaves were likely the dominant factors which propelled' the abolition issue. She gives three economic factors which negatively affected the

Caribbean plantation economy. Looking specifically at the British Virgin Islands, she finds five reasons why it was no longer viable to maintain slavery as an economic mode of production.

141 **The long march to freedom: a glimpse at the Virgin Islands.**
Norwell Harrigan. Road Town, Tortola: Laurel, 1985. 20p.
A brief but masterful study of slavery in the Virgin Islands. It assesses human progress from slavery to emancipation, from colonial administration to the present period of autonomy and economic boom. Political, cultural and social themes are interwoven and the author exposes the problems and dangers he foresees for the future. This work is considered to be necessary reading for a wide range of scholars.

142 **One hundred and fifty years of achievement, 1834-1984.**
Edited by Eileen Parsons. Road Town, Tortola: Education Department, 1984. 153p.
This significant work 'sheds light on the achievements and abilities of British Virgin Islanders hitherto unhonoured and unsung'. A number of knowledgeable Virgin Islanders contributed to this volume in the 150th year after emancipation. It consists of historical writing about educators, sea captains, boat-builders, sportsmen, doctors and grannies, rum distillers, food and crafts. Some creative writing and old-time sayings are also included. Contributors include Dr N. Harrigan, E. Scatliffe, V. Penn Moll, Iris Fahie, E. Todman-Smith, E. Glasgow, Q. Lettsome, A. Turnbull, and I. Hodge.

143 **The slave rebellion of 1823 in Tortola, British Virgin Islands.**
Michael O'Neal. St. Thomas: University of the Virgin Islands and Virgin Islands Historical Society, Nov. 1987. 29p.
The socio-historical context of the slave uprising is highlighted. Published as part of the *Proceedings of a conference on slavery and emancipation in the Virgin Islands*.

144 **The trial of Arthur Hodge.**
A.M. Belisario. London: J. Harding, 1811. 145p.
An account of the incidents which led to the hanging of a colonial planter for the murder of one of his slaves in the British Virgin Islands. It is the classic case of justice for slaves, which set a precedent in the entire Caribbean, and possibly in the world.

# Virgin Islands, US

145 **America's Virgin Islands: a history of human rights and wrongs.**
William W. Boyer. Durham, North Carolina: Carolina Academic Press, 1983. 418p. maps. bibliog.
The reality of slavery, prejudice, poverty and prosperity in the islands, is presented in 3 parts – Roots: 1492-1917; Freedom Struggle: 1917-1954; Tourism Syndrome: 1954-1980. It is a very readable piece of documentation by an internationally recognized scholar of development in less-developed countries. Boyer travels, advises and lectures in Asian, European and other countries; he is professor of Public Administration at the University of Delaware. There are useful tables and an index.

146  **Eyewitness accounts of slavery in the Danish West Indian Islands.**
Isidor Paiewonsky, designed by Barry Eisenberg.    [n.p.], USA:
The author, 1987. 166p.

A brilliant presentation by an author who is widely recognized for his extraordinary lifelong achievement as businessman, humanitarian and historian of his native Virgin Islands. 'It is more than a study of time and place; it is an historical document of man's inhumanity to man.'

147  **Night of the silent drums.**
John L. Anderson.    New York: Charles Scribner's Sons, 1975. 406p.

Set in St. John, United States Virgin Islands, the narrative enacts for us the agony and the urgency of a slave revolt in the eighteenth century.

148  **Report of the execrable conspiracy carried out by the Amino negroes in the Danish Island of St. Jan in America in 1733.**
Pierre J. Pannet, translated and edited by Aimery P. Caron, Arnold R. Highfield.    Christiansted, St. Croix: Antilles Press, 1984. 23p. maps.

Inspiration for this reprint came from the 250th anniversary of the slave rebellion in St. John. Lavish illustrations and text notes help to explain the conspiracy in greater detail.

# Plantations

## Virgin Islands, UK

149  **Afro-Caribbean villages in historical perspective.**
Edited by Charles V. Carnegie.    Kingston, Jamaica: African
Caribbean Institute, 1987. 133p.

The historical development of particular Caribbean communities is the central theme of this book. It is a collection of case-studies which provides an invaluable methodological tool, opening up to scrutiny the history and organization of village communites in the Caribbean. Contributors Sidney W. Mintz, Karen Fog Olwig, Trevor Purcell, O. Nigel Bollard, Charles Carnegie and Jean Besson share a common concern: to understand African cultural continuities within the dynamic social context of the Caribbean communities in which they took on new life and significance. The facts which Karen Fog Olwig reveals in the paper, 'Village, culture and identity on St. John, Virgin Islands', p. 20-44, are true down to the minutest detail.

150  **British Virgin Islands plantation society.**
Michael O'Neal.    Charlotte Amalie, St. Thomas: Caribbean Studies
Association, 1981. 22p.

Some aspects of the social relations of production in the plantation society of the British Virgin Islands are presented in this paper which was delivered at the sixth annual conference of the Caribbean Studies Association, held on 27-30 May 1981.

151 **The decline of the sugar plantations on Tortola, British Virgin Islands, 1775-1834.**
Emma Wallace. [n.p.]: [n.p.], [n.d.]. 50p. map. bibliog.

This brief work covers the economy of sugar, the organization of a sugar plantation, and makes a comparison of plantations in the late 19th century and early 20th centuries. It concludes that 'although the sugar era [on Tortola] spanned considerably less years than that of other islands, lasting for little more than half a century, yet it played a major role in shaping British Virgin Islands history'. Unfortunately neither the name of the publisher nor the date of publication appears anywhere in the book.

152 **Marginality and flux: an Afro-Caribbean community through three centuries.**
Frank S. McGlynn. PhD thesis, University of Pittsburgh, Pittsburgh, 1980. 135p. maps. bibliog.

The focus is on the village of Long Look, the oldest Afro-Caribbean freed community in the English-speaking Caribbean. It analyses the village through the periods of slavery, 1770-1830; post emancipation, 1830-70; peasantry, 1870-1900; and the 20th century. The author seeks to explore the interplay of social relationships at community level as they respond to historical events. There are five maps, several tables and seven appendixes. This work is a contribution to the people of the Virgin Islands and of the Caribbean, by a dedicated anthropologist. (Now available from University Microfilms International, Ann Arbor, Michigan, 48106).

# Virgin Islands, US

153 **The Bordeaux Plantation, 1685-1973.**
Enid Baa. Charlotte Amalie, St. Thomas: Conference of Caribbean Historians, 1978. 62p.

The paper is about some aspects of the activities surrounding the esteemed and privileged Brandenburgers in St. Thomas, and some personalities who were involved with Estate Bordeaux, the seat of the Brandenburg plantation. It was presented at the tenth conference of Caribbean Historians.

154 **The Enighed estate and ruin of St. John, United States Virgin Islands.**
George F. Tyson. Charlotte Amalie, St. Thomas: Island Resources Foundation, 1976. 47p.

This little work is an excellent historical survey with tremendous scholarly input, much of the research for its accomplishment having been done in Denmark, a former colonizer of the United States Virgin Islands. It is a source of tremendous value for explaining and identifying old ruins on the island of St. John.

# Population

## General

155 **Demographic yearbook.**
Department of Economic and Social Affairs. Statistical Office. New York: United Nations, 1948- . annual.

This yearbook carries statistics on population in almost every country in the world. Categories of figures include birth and death rates, migration, marriages and related issues, and the composition of households. According to preliminary data released from the Census Office of the Development Planning Unit in the British Virgin Islands, News Release no. 149R/91 (19 August 1991), p. 1-2, the 1992-93 volume of the *Demographic yearbook* should show an increase of 40 per cent in the British Virgin Islands population – figures have risen from 12,034 in 1980 to 17,773 in 1991.

## Virgin Islands, UK

156 **Demographic and economic assumptions and strategies for the British Virgin Islands national physical development plan.**
Ralph Kaminsky. [n.p.]: United Nations Development Programme, 1976. 17p.

This document analyses the territory's demographic assets and other resources and offers strategies for economic planning and for formulating national development plans.

157  **1980-1991 population census of the Commonwealth Caribbean: British Virgin Islands, volume one.**
Regional Census Co-ordinating Committee, with foreword by Hubert Barker.   [n.p.]: Caricom Council of Ministers, 1980. 101p.
Scores of tabulation figures give the demographic details of the territory. The population is tabulated by sex, age group and enumeration district and in another instance the population is shown by major division, single years of age and sex. On pages 16-46, the economic activity of the population aged fifteen years and over, is shown. Other sections indicate the position of immigration; education; vocational training; race and religion; marital and union status and fertility; housing; services and the household arrangements of the territory. A sample of the questionnaire used is appended. The work is the joint effort of the Regional Census Co-ordinating Committee and the national office of the British Virgin Islands. The United Nations Fund for Population Activities provided financial support for the processing and printing phases of the programme. It is a herculean effort and a work of lasting value.

**British Virgin Islands: territorial report for the year 1987.**
*See* item no. 9.

**Treasure islands: a guide to the British Virgin Islands.**
*See* item no. 13.

**British Virgin Islands Tourist Handbook, 1990.**
*See* item no. 69.

**The Virgin Islands story.**
*See* item no. 126.

**The long march to freedom: a glimpse at the Virgin Islands.**
*See* item no. 141.

**Culture, race and class in the Commonwealth Caribbean.**
*See* item no. 197.

**Social structure of the British Caribbean.**
*See* item no. 198.

**Development, immigration and politics in a pre-industrial society: a study of social change in the British Virgin Islands in the 1960s.**
*See* item no. 200.

**Social and economic review no. 3.**
*See* item no. 289.

# Nationalities and minorities

## Virgin Islands, UK and US

158 **Caribbean ethnicity revisited.**
Edited by Stephen Glazier. New York; London; Paris; Tokyo: Gordon and Breach, 1985. 164p.

This timely selection of papers by a number of eminent anthropologists, explores the patterns of ethnicity in the Caribbean, and provides a fascinating and vital study of the region as a whole. Klaus de Albuquerque and Jerome L. McElroy's paper, 'Race and ethnicity in the United States Virgin Islands' (p. 41-70), analyses patterns of race and ethnic relations in the islands since they were transferred in 1917 from Denmark to the United States. Attention is given to the structure and behaviour of major ethnic groups: French and Puerto Ricans, immigrant whites and blacks from the US mainland and West Indians from the surrounding Eastern Caribbean.

159 **Estimated composition of Virgin Islands population by groups, 1950, 1960, 1965.**
Martin Garson Orlins. In: *The impact of tourism on the Virgin Islands of the United States*, PhD dissertation, Columbia University, 1969, p. 324-5, 331, 339.

Orlins defines native Virgin Islanders and suggests that around 1950, at the introduction of tourism, they numbered between 66 and 75 per cent of the insular population. By 1965, however, they comprised less than half of the total, and 'every population group in the Islands represented a minority group'. The table lists figures for the fifteen-year period for five categories: natives, aliens, Puerto Ricans, Old French and continentals.

160 **A French community on St. Thomas.**
Warren T. Morill, Bennet Dyke. *Caribbean Studies*, vol. 5. no. 4 (Jan. 1966), p. 39-47.

A preliminary report of research carried out on the French-speaking communities of St. Thomas, United States Virgin Islands. It finds that the population is divided into two communities: Carenage and North Side. The North Side French have shifted from subsistence farming and fishing to wage labour as a main source of income. Despite this, they preserve marked cultural and social similarities with the parent population of St. Barthelemy.

161 **Institutional and societal bases of rural development: two French 'villages' on St. Thomas, Virgin Islands.**
Simon G. Jones-Hendrickson. St. Thomas: Caribbean Research Institute, 143p. maps.

The study seeks to 'understand why there has been a social cohesion among the two communities in the Virgin Islands in what is an otherwise "fluid" society in the Virgin Islands'. Both societies migrated from St. Barts, West Indies – one from a fishing village, the other from an agricultural one.

162 **The Jews of the Virgin Islands.**
Alexander Alland. *American Hebrew*, vol. 146, no. 20 (19 March 1940), p. 12-16; vol. 156, no. 21 (5 April 1940), p. 6-7; vol. 146, no. 24 (26 April 1940), p. 12-13.
In this sequence of articles, Alland outlines candid biographies of outstanding Jews born on St. Thomas, United States Virgin Islands.

163 **The Puerto Rico migrant in St. Croix.**
Clarence Senior. Rio Piedras, Puerto Rico: Social Science Research Centre, University of Puerto Rico, 1947. 42p.
Outlines the history of Puerto Ricans living in St. Croix, United States Virgin Islands, and assesses their assimilation and standing – social, economic and political – in the community.

164 **Race relations in Puerto Rico and the Virgin Islands.**
Eric E. Williams. *Foreign Affairs*, vol. 23, no. 2 (Jan. 1945), p. 308-17.
An internationally recognized historian analyses the preferences and attitudes of various ethnic groupings· firstly in one of the largest Caribbean islands and then in a much smaller area, the United States Virgin Islands.

165 **Virgin Islands English creoles.**
Gilbert Sprave. [n.p.]: Caribbean Research Institute, 1977, p. 8-28. (Microstate Studies, one).
The author offers some chronological considerations relating to the arrival and existence of English creoles, an ethnic group residing in St. Thomas, United States Virgin Islands.

**A history of the Virgin Islands of the United States.**
*See* item no. 130.

**America's Virgin Islands: a history of human rights and wrongs.**
*See* item no. 145.

**Cultural aspects of delusion: a psychiatric study of the Virgin Islands.**
*See* item no. 226.

**Economic Review.**
*See* item no. 576.

**Virgin Islands Labour Market Review.**
*See* item no. 592.

# Immigration

## Virgin Islands, UK

166 **Customs and immigration in the British Virgin Islands.**
Edited by John Scott Fones, coordinated by Elihu Rhymer. In: *Doing Business in the British Virgin Islands.* Road Town, Tortola: British Virgin Islands Tourist Board, [n.d.]. 8p.

A handy summary of Customs regulations pertaining to visitors and the import of commercial goods is given. Immigration is similarly treated with the emphasis on visitors' and residents' requirements for entering and staying in the country.

167 **Customs and immigration seminar.**
Government Information Service. *News Release*, vol. 102R/91 (29 May 1991), p. 1-2.

According to this issue, a five-day seminar for Customs and Immigration staffs was conducted by Roosevelt Finlayson of the Bahamas-based consultancy firm, Management Development Resources, in Road Town, Tortola. Elements of the seminar included 'an evaluation of the impact of culture on service attitudes, team building techniques, the components of excellent service and the improvement of self image'. The proceedings of the seminar should be useful to anyone studying immigration and customs in a tourist economy. Information may be obtained from the Government Information Service, Road Town, Tortola, British Virgin Islands.

# Migration

168 **Eastern Caribbean migrants in the United States of America: a demographic profile.**
Averille White. *Bulletin of Eastern Caribbean Affairs*, vol. 13, no. 4 (Sept.-Oct. 1976). p. 8-28.

The demographic characteristics of the Eastern Caribbean migrants to the United States of America are described. Information includes: country of birth; year of migration; age; educational attainment and employment status. Data also show that although most migrants of Eastern Caribbean origin are employed, only a small proportion of persons hold professional occupations. It is interesting to note that the United States Virgin Islanders are considered citizens of the United States of America and are therefore not included in this grouping. British Virgin Islanders on the other hand are included; 1,867 British Virgin Islanders migrated between 1975 and 1980.

# Virgin Islands, US

169  **United States immigration and naturalization service.**
Majorie Roberts.   *Pride*, vol. 8, no. 12 (Dec. 1989), p. 17, 34.

Roberts explains the status of the 'alien' in the Virgin Islands and the various types of non-immigrant and immigrant visas for which they may apply. The requirements and benefits of each are spelt out as well as the larger benefits which 'naturalization' (i.e. full citizenship) can bestow.

# Language and Dialects

## General

**170  Caribbean and African languages: social history, language and literature and education.**
Morgan Dalphines.  London: Karia, 1985. 288p. bibliog.
Topics such as social history of creole languages, oral literature, the teaching of English as a second language and creole in adult education are discussed with conviction and enthusiasm. Recommendations are also made for a productive use of creole languages in teaching.

## Virgin Islands, UK

**171  Bohog putin gol' teet'.**
Road Town, Tortola: British Virgin Islands High School, Language Department, [n.d.]. 28p.
Further work on a school project entitled 'Proverbial Expressions' was accelerated when the Public Library sponsored a competition on 'Ole Time Sayings'; this is the result of the combined effort of the staff and students. The expressions and their meanings are grouped into sections: 'A person's place in society'; 'Relationships'; 'Advice'; 'Attitude'; and 'Miscellaneous'. There is a pronunciation guide, and the artwork in pen and ink was done by Meston Malone.

# Virgin Islands, US

172 **Herbs and proverbs of the Virgin Islands.**
Arona Petersen. Charlotte Amalie, St. Thomas: St. Thomas
Graphics, 1975. 78p.

Charmingly illustrated, this special collection of proverbs and wise sayings comes from
the pen of a herbalist. Quite naturally therefore there is some emphasis on sayings
about local herbs, including an amusing section about 'the bush bath'. There is also a
glossary of terms used.

173 **Het negerhollands der Deese Antillean: bijdrage tot de geschiedenis der
Nederlandse Taal in America.** (The negro Dutch of the Danish Antilles:
contribution to the history of the Dutch language in America.)
D.C. Hesseling. Leiden, The Netherlands: Sijthoff, 1905. 270p.

The negro, with a rich background of African languages, the oral tradition and an
amazing ability to adapt and improvise in conversation and story-telling, played an
important part in the metamorphosis of language. This very important early document
emphasizes that invaluable contribution.

174 **Ole time sayings.**
Lito Valls. St. John: Valls, 1983. [n.p.]. bibliog.

These include proverbs of the West Indies as a whole but the emphasis is on the Virgin
Islands proverbs. The items are numbered and the index refers to each one by a
number. There is a useful glossary.

175 **Riddle me one, riddle me two.**
Jan Kallaloo (pseud., Lito Valls). St. John: Valls, [n.d.]. 34p.

These island riddles are witty and funny; there is an adequate glossary for the
uninitiated.

# Dictionaries of Creole

176 **Virgin Islands dictionary.**
George A. Seaman. St. Croix: [n.p.], 1976. 4th rev. ed. Originally
published in 1967. 20p.

In this revised and enlarged Creole–English dictionary, the author has caught the
rhythms of the creole dialects to which he has added his own sensitive interpretations.
However, no etymology or idiomatic background of the words and phrases is given.
Examples of entries include: 'Barna: One's behind or rear; Bazady: Mentally
unbalanced, crazy; Bittle: To beat, to chastise'.

**177 What a pistarcle: a dictionary of Virgin Islands English Creole.**
Lito Valls.   St. John: Valls, 1981. 139p.

The entries give meanings and examples of usage; they explore the origins of over 200 words and phrases. Although United States Virgin Islands' usage is more prevalent, there are many words common to the composite Virgin group. This is an authoritative and well cross-referenced work which benefits from the author's experience; previously he was an educator and librarian, and is now a historian with the Virgin Islands National Park, St. John, United States Virgin Islands. A supplement consisting of seventy-four pages of additional words and terms was published in 1990. They are available from: Environmental Studies Program, Inc., PO Box 84, Cruz Bay, St. John, United States Virgin Islands, 00830.

# Folklore

## Virgin Islands, UK

178  **Folklore in the Virgin Islands.**
Verna Penn.  *Island Sun* (27 Oct. 1979), p. 8.
The article defines folklore and its origin in the islands. It traces early sources and emphasizes that 'cultural focus pivoting around folklore in all its manifestations' has much to say which is relevant to the development of the commercial and economic interests of the islands.

179  **The folklore of the British Virgin Islands.**
Trevor Bates.  Cambridge, England: Cambridge University Press, [n.d.]. 509p. maps.
This study is one of the earliest about the culture of the islands; it is detailed and important. It looks at the islands' history; the people and church; the work-a-day world; the occult and the uncanny; pregnancy, birth and childhood; sex, courtship and marriage; death, wakes and burial; folk beliefs and folk literature. There are several interesting folk photos which are also of historical interest; these include a boys' orchestra, scenes of Road Town and St. John. There are appendixes on: tales from Anegada, St. John and Tortola; proverbs from St. John and Tortola; riddles of St. John and Tortola. The work also has a glossary of vernacular terms, notes and references.

# Virgin Islands, US

180 **Folklife fest: V.I. in luck.**
   Anna Mae Brown. *Daily News*, 18 April 1990, p. 10.
This guest editorial describes the purpose of the annual Festival of American Folklife which was established in 1967 by the Smithsonian Institution. The writer is the coordinator for the Virgin Islands contribution to the Smithsonian Folklife Festival.

**Divers information on the romantic history of St. Croix: from the time of Columbus until today.**
*See* item no. 128.

**In Danish times.**
*See* item no. 131.

**Cultural aspects of delusion: a psychiatric study of the Virgin Islands.**
*See* item no. 226.

# Religion

## General

**181  Caribbean Quakers.**
Harriet Frorer Durham.    Hollywood, Florida: Dukane, 1972. 133p.
maps. bibliog.

An overview of the history of the Quakers in the West Indies. It begins in 1650 and traces the Quakers' arrival, successes and trials up to the present day. The book is based on earlier comprehensive works and some original materials. One chapter (p. 57-78), in which fact and fiction are presented, is devoted to the British Virgin Islands. Much space is given to disproving anecdotes.

**182  Real roots and potted plants: reflections on the Caribbean Church.**
Ashley Smith.    Williamsfield, Jamaica: Mandeville, 1984. 91p.

This collection of papers delivered over a thirteen-year span analyses the effectiveness of the Church's ministry to the Caribbean people. The author emphasizes the need for people to break free of the forces of spiritual enslavement, and he addresses the Church's task in social change and renewal, justice and development, liberation, faith and economics, changing systems and hope. This book is a critical look at the Church in the emergent Caribbean by a qualified and experienced insider who lectures at the Theological College of the West Indies, Jamaica. It is applicable to the entire Caribbean including the British and United States Virgin Islands where religion was imported, largely wholesale.

183  **Souvenir booklet giving thanks to God for the Conference of the Methodist Church in the Caribbean and the Americas celebrating its 21st Meeting.**
Belmont, Antigua: Methodist Church in the Caribbean and the Americas, 1987. 51p.

Twenty years of Methodism in the Caribbean, run by the region's own Conference, instead of the London Methodist Missionary Society, is no mean achievement. Reflections of forty-two Caribbean men of God on the development of a significant Conference make informative and soul-stirring reading. One of John Wesley's quotations – 'the best of all is God is with us' – crests of the Conference and Church, and photographs of the headquarters of the Conference in Antigua embellish the cover.

# Virgin Islands, UK

184  **Anglicans to mark Silver Year of churches merger.**
*British Virgin Island Beacon*, vol. 5, no. 23 (17 Nov. 1988), p. 4, 6.

Reports on the celebratory plans for recognizing the anniversary of the transfer of the Anglican Church of the British Virgin Islands from the Diocese of Antigua to the Episcopal Church of the United States. This is one of the peculiar incidences in the Virgin Islands, when two different political jurisdictions merge their forces into one.

185  **Annual Synod, 1980.**
Methodist Church.   Road Town, Tortola: British Virgin Islands Circuit, 1980. 32p.

A record of the activities, programmes and personalities associated with the Synod held in the British Virgin Islands from 28 January to 9 February 1980. The illustrations of persons and places are of lasting historic value.

186  **East End Methodist Church: 175th anniversary, 1810-1985.**
V.E. Moll.   East End, Tortola: East End Methodist Church, 1985. 25p.

This booklet surveys the history and development of the oldest standing Methodist Church building in the Virgin Islands. It includes brief articles and messages from past ministers now living across the Caribbean, in England and in America; lists of missionaries, ministers and officers who served from 1789 to 1985; a chronology of highlights of the 20th century, and a glossary of religious symbols.

187  **Formation of the British Virgin Islands Christian Council.**
*Island Sun*, no. 1610 (13 April 1991), p. 11.

The reported objectives of the Christian Council are: to provide fellowship among the clergy; to provide a means by which the churches may take council together; to study the problems and opportunities which challenge the Christian way of life; to promote cooperative action when it is necessary; and to air the spiritual issues involved in community problems in the light of Christian ideals and standards.

188   **Methodism: two hundred years in the British Virgin Islands.**
      Francis Woodie Blackman.   Bridgetown, Barbados: Methodist Church British Virgin Islands, 1989. 151p. map.

This record of joyous achievement is presented in two parts. Part one deals with the early years of Methodism in the islands; responsibility and progress; Methodism and slavery; post-emancipation consolidation; United Brethren (Moravians) and Methodism; some vicissitudes; administration – past and present; 20th-century challenge and change; church and school, further challenge and service. Part two gives an account of some chapels and societies; some servants of God; and the church and materialism. The appendixes are important: a copy of a memorial from the Wesleyan Mission House to the Secretary of State; a list of Methodist missionaries who served in Tortola, 1788-1885; circuit officers and local preachers. The work is illustrated, and the notes and index make it an invaluable document of research and inspiration.

189   **Tortola: a Quaker experiment of long ago in the tropics.**
      Charles F. Jenkins.   London: Friends Bookshop, 1923. 106p. maps.

The history of the Quaker movement in Tortola, covering a period of forty-five years. It records the birth, activity, decline and death of the Tortola episode but it also contains useful documents and important maps dealing with various aspects of the island's history.

**Early history of the British Virgin Islands: from Columbus to emancipation.**
*See* item no. 121.

**The Virgin Islands story.**
*See* item no. 126.

# Virgin Islands, US

190   **Annual Synod, 1987.**
      St. Thomas: Methodist Church in the Caribbean and the Americas, 1987. 52p.

Every year some Caribbean country experiences the annual Methodist Synod which is usually both a challenge and a delight. The booklet consists of inspirational messages, pictorial biographies of the clergy, a list of delegates and a rousing historical account of the local Christ Church of St. Thomas.

191 **Historic churches of the Virgin Islands.**
William Chapman, W. Taylor, foreword by Frederick Gjessing. St.
Croix: Landmarks Society, [n.d.].
This splendid volume presents a varied representation of churches of different religious
denominations. Clear and illuminating, it sets off the architectural gender of the
islands. The work is appropriately illustrated, the cover being designed by William
Taylor.

192 **The history of the African Methodist Episcopal Church in the Virgin
Islands.**
Veneta Adams-Gordon. *Missionary*, vol. 65, no. 2 (Feb. 1963),
p. 10-11.
The article centres on this Church's concentration on the island of St. Croix, United
States Virgin Islands, and assesses its impact on the morals and social development of
that society.

193 **Praise God: two hundred years (1773-1973): history of the Catholic
Church in St. Thomas.**
Edited by John Gauci. Charlotte Amalie, St. Thomas: Redemptorist
Fathers, 1973. 77p.
An important compendium of religious history by experts on the subject. Articles
include: 'Catholicism in the Caribbean', by Enid Baa; 'The Catholic Church of St.
Thomas, Virgin Islands, its early history' by Jos G. Daly; 'The Immaculate
Conception' by Cyril Michael; and 'Decade of chance' by John Gauci.

194 **Preservation of the Sephardic records of the island of St. Thomas,
Virgin Islands.**
Enid Baa. *Publication of American Jewish Historical Society*, vol. 44,
no. 2 (Dec. 1954), p. 114-19.
The article describes how the Synagogue records on St. Thomas, Virgin Islands, were
preserved and classified. It also recognizes the contribution which early Jews made to
the commercial life of the islands.

195 **Religious development.**
Enid Baa. In: *Fifty years: commemorating the fiftieth anniversary of
the transfer of the Virgin Islnds from Denmark to the United States of
America March 31, 1967*, edited by Ernest Downing. Charlotte
Amalie, St. Thomas: Friends of Denmark Society, 1967, p. 45-57.
The article outlines the introduction and development of religion in the Danish West
Indies. It briefly deals with the Roman Catholic, Lutheran, Dutch Reformed,
Moravian, Jewish and Anglican religions.

**Religion.** Virgin Islands, US

196 **Virgin Islands story: a history of the Lutheran State Church, other churches, slavery, education and culture in the Danish West Indies, now the Virgin Islands.**
Peter M. Jens Larsen.   Philadelphia, Pennsylvania: Muhlenberg, 1950. 250p. bibliog.
This is essential reading for anyone studying the religion and social history of the islands. Illustrations and footnotes add authenticity and interest.

**A history of the Virgin Islands of the United States.**
*See* item no. 122.

**In Danish times.**
*See* item no. 131.

**The Jews of the Virgin Islands.**
*See* item no. 162.

# Social Structure

## General

**197  Culture, race and class in the Commonwealth Caribbean.**

M.G. Smith, with a foreword by Rex Nettleford.   Mona, Jamaica:
Department of Extra-mural Studies, University of the West Indies,
1984. 163p.

Smith reviews various accounts of Anglo-Caribbean societies from 1945 to the present,
and discusses the parts that culture, race and class play in them. The work seeks to
assess the collective contribution of these studies and to clarify the critical issues and
relations with which they deal. Although attention focuses on four West Indian
societies, the book also presents general models which could be applied to the Virgin
Islands for they are also of that 'distinctive socio-eco order determined by experiences
and historical formation rooted in the chattle slavery and plantation system'.

**198  Social structure of the British Caribbean.**

George Cumber.   Millwood, New York: Kraus Reprint, 1978. 90p.

A thorough treatment of the subject which deals with topics such as population and
vital statistics of the British West Indies in general, and individual islands in particular;
inter-colonial immigration; housing and racial groups. There is much tabulated
information with historical comparisons; for example, the population table on page 9
includes census figures for the British Virgin Islands: in 1871 the population was 6,651
and in 1946 it was 6,505. Table 2 shows the gainfully employed population by industry
groups and colonies and another table indicates colonial immigration by age and sex.
Originally published by the Extra-mural Department of the University of the West
Indies, this is recommended reading for anyone who wishes to gain an insight into the
general background of the social structure of the islands.

199 **Welfare and planning in the West Indies.**
T.S. Simey. Oxford: Clarendon Press, 1946. 267p. map.
The origins, organization, economic foundations and the rebuilding of West Indian society are the engaging topics discussed in this work. The section on 'social welfare schemes' refers (on pages 127-8) to a development plan for the United States Virgin Islands, developed by the Caribbean Field Office of Natural Resources Planning Board of Puerto Rico. It includes results of inquiries into vital statistics, the cost of living, land use, and economic organization.

# Virgin Islands, UK

200 **Development, immigration and politics in a pre-industrial society: a study of social change in the British Virgin Islands in the 1960s.**
W. Errol Bowen. *Caribbean Studies*, vol. 16, no. 1 (April 1976), p. 67-85.
The article looks at the social repercussions caused by the interplay of three sets of changes: the decade of starting development in the islands and transformation from their pre-industrial state; the large influx of immigrants from the Caribbean and the United Kingdom; and the transition from the old-style colonial administration to representative-style politics.

201 **A profile of social development in the British Virgin Islands.**
Norwell Harrigan. *Caribbean Studies*. vol. 10, no. 4 (Jan. 1971), p. 75-92.
This stalwart scholar discusses social development up to the 1960s and concludes that development must come from the bottom up, using techniques to stimulate initiatives, self-help and mutual help.

202 **The second actuarial review of the Social Security scheme.**
Hermando Perez Montas and Associates. Road Town, Tortola: Social Security Board, 1988. 36p.
The review speaks well of the performance of the Social Security scheme and makes recommendations accordingly. Four outstanding ones reflect increases in payments: an increase of maternity grant from $75 USC to $150 USC; an increase of the funeral grant from $200 USC to $700 USC; an increase on rate of sickness benefit from 60 per cent to 66.6 per cent of average insurable earnings of the sick individual; and a ceiling on insurable earnings from $10,800 USC to $13,800 USC.

203  **A symposium for social change: implications for the British Virgin Islands.**
Road Town, Tortola: British Virgin Islands Mental Health Association. 1982. 31p.

Every year, a week is set aside to address the problems of the mental health of the British Virgin Islands community. The question of social change and its impact on the society are thoroughly examined by persons expert in the fields of sociology, anthropology, mental health and psychiatry. This issue records some actions which could be taken to relieve certain pressures on individuals and groups in the community.

**British Virgin Islands: territorial report for the year 1987.**
*See* item no. 9.

**The Virgin Islands story.**
*See* item no. 126.

**1980-1991 population census of the Commonwealth Caribbean: British Virgin Islands, volume one.**
*See* item no. 157.

**Caribbean ethnicity revisited.**
*See* item no. 158.

**Social and economic review no. 3.**
*See* item no. 289.

**Housing programmes and policies in the British Virgin Islands: a perspective for twenty-eight years (1973-2000).**
*See* item no. 393.

# Virgin Islands, US

204  **Leaflets from the Danish West Indies.**
C. Edwin Taylor, with a biographical sketch of the author by P. Linet.   Westport, Connecticut: Negro University Press, 1988. 208p.

A detailed description of the social, political and commercial condition of these islands.

205  **Social networks in St. Croix, United States Virgin Islands.**
James W. Green.   PhD thesis, University of Washington, Washington DC, 1972. 378p.

A thorough analysis of the interplay of major historical events and the development of social and cultural patterns in St. Croix. There is much ethnographic detail, especially regarding male and female relationships, although primarily from a male point of view. The role of the matrifocal family is assessed against the background of slavery, colonization and emancipation.

## Problems

206   **Trouble in Paradise.**
Les Payna.   *Black Enterprise*, vol. 8 (March 1981), p. 40-4.
Payna claims in this illustrated article that the 'United States Virgin Islands are torn by racial and economic tensions which contradict their image as America's playland'.

**The history of the Virgin Islands of the United States.**
*See* item no. 130.

**Trials and triumphs: the big road to a middle class society in the United States Virgin Islands.**
*See* item no. 135.

**The United States Virgin Islands.**
*See* item no. 136.

**Caribbean ethnicity revisited.**
*See* item no. 158.

**The Virgin Islands approach to housing and community development.**
*See* item no. 397.

**Directory of Human Services.**
*See* item no. 599.

# Social services

## Virgin Islands, UK

207   **Social Development Department: annual report for the year 1988.**
Social Development Department.   Road Town, Tortola: British Virgin Islands Government, 1989. 40p.
Administration, social welfare services, Adina Donovan Home, youth development activities, community development activities, and sports are the six sections under which the entire operation of the department is discussed. The report sees the department as 'a catalyst for social change working with the people of the British Virgin Islands community to assist in identifying felt needs and to assist in designing strategies to meet those needs'. Among the several changes it records, is the added responsibility of the administration of the Adina Donovan Home for the Elderly (originally managed by the Medical and Health Department). Recommendations on page 39 reflect the problems of the department: that appropriate numbers of personnel be provided to address the social ills of the Territory; that adequate office space be provided to accommodate the necessary number of staff members; and that adequate

funds be provided for programmes suitable to needs, particularly in the area of youth development. Tables of statistics which help to verify the text make this an indispensable reference source on social development aspects of the country.

208 **Study confronts garbage disposal problems.**
Kenneth Clark. *British Virgin Island Beacon*, vol. 5. no. 7 (21 July 1988), p. 5, 12.
According to Bill Walker from the Canadian environmental consulting firm, M.M. Dillon, the study on garbage disposal and sewerage treatment conducted in the British Virgin Islands emphasized in its report the importance of training local people to operate and maintain the essential equipment which has to be recommended. Another recommendation is 'that the legislation be modified to specify holding tanks for yachts and to specify dumping stations for them, not in the open water'. When completed, the study will be available from the Public Health Department, Road Town, Tortola, British Virgin Islands.

# Virgin Islands, US

209 **Department of Human Services: annual report, 1988 and 1989.**
Department of Human Sciences. St. Thomas: Virgin Islands of the United States Government, 1990. 45p.
The history of human services in the United States Virgin Islands is outlined and six accomplishments are highlighted in the summary for the period under review. These include: the conducting of a series of neighbourhood improvement projects in which over 700 youngsters participated; a summer fest programme on all three islands to promote a drug-free Virgin Islands; and the establishing of an employment assistance programme through which nine employees and their families received assistance.

210 **Virgin Islands household survey.**
Cora L. Christian. Charlotte Amalie, St. Thomas: Department of Health, 1988. [n.p.].
This aggregation of facts and figures is an important source of social and medical data. Dr Christian, who was also the director and chief investigator of the survey, has illustrated how the information could be used to diagnose and assess health and social needs in the community. A paper entitled 'Prevalence of elevated blood pressure in children' and drawing on some of the results of the survey was published in *Ethnicity and Disease* by Loyola University Stritch School of Medicine, USA in January 1991. There is little doubt that this useful source will continue to generate publications, interest and action in the medical and related communities both in the Virgin Islands and further afield for a long time to come. Dr Christian is Assistant Commissioner of Health in the Virgin Islands, a consultant for the Pan-American Health Organization (PAHO), and a keen researcher who lectures extensively throughout the Caribbean and the United States of America.

211 **Directory of services for the elderly.**
Charlotte Amalie, St. Thomas: Community Action Agency, 1977.
102p.
A reference aid which contains useful information about services available for the elderly.

# Medicine and Health

## General

**212 Afro-Caribbean folk medicine.**
Michel S. Laguerre. [n.p.], Massachusetts: Garvey, 1987. 120p. bibliog.
This important study analyses and puts some conceptual order into the vast domain of
Caribbean folk beliefs and practices. Among the topics it covers are: the evolution of
slave medicine; transmission of folk medicine knowledge; the practitioners; body,
blood and illness and faith healing. There are four useful appendixes: A sample of
African plants brought to the Caribbean by slave ships; Medicinal plants used by
Caribbean slaves; Food items with hot and cold qualities; and A sample of medicinal
plants used in the Caribbean. Fifteen Caribbean islands are analysed, the author thus
providing a better understanding of a persisting folk medicine tradition which is not
generally known. He is the Associate Professor of Caribbean Studies at the University
of California.

**213 Commonwealth Caribbean Medical Resource Council: proceedings of a
scientific meeting.**
Kingston, Jamaica: West Indian Medical Research Council, 1989. 84p.
The supplement to the *West Indian Medical Journal* records the deliberations of a
meeting held on 19-22 April 1989. It includes a list of on-going research topics and
reports on new medical trends in the region.

**214 Teenage pregnancy in the Caribbean.**
Tirbani Jagdeo. New York: Inter-American Parliamentary Group on
Population and Development, 1985. 12p.
Deals generally with the situation of family planning in the Caribbean and presents a
plea for action.

# Virgin Islands, UK

215 **Aims and objectives of British Virgin Islands Council on Alcohol and Drug Abuse.**
British Virgin Islands Council on Alcohol and Abuse. *CANA Newsletter*, no. 8 (June 1987), p. 3.
The Council's aims and objectives are clearly set out thus: To eliminate the stigma associated with alcohol and drug addiction; To raise community awareness of alcohol related problems; To establish primary prevention programmes for youth and high-risk groups; and To establish consultation and referral services for anyone troubled by alcohol and other drugs. A similar problem in the US Virgin Islands is tackled in *Achieving drug free schools: a policy for use in the schools of the Virgin Islands* (Foreword by Linda Creque. Charlotte Amalie, St. Thomas: Department of Education, 1989. 12p.), a guide to interpreting the school drugs policy which was approved by the Joint Boards of Education on 24 February 1989. It is 'an effective response to potential and current use and abuse of alcohol and drugs by members of the school population'. The policy sets out 'the courses of action required by educational personnel encountering alcohol and other drug abuse problems on school premises or school sponsored activities'.

216 **Doctors find treatment for fish poisoning.**
*British Virgin Island Beacon*, vol. 5. no. 7 (21 July 1988), p. 7.
Virgin Islands and Caribbean doctors, according to this report, have in 'mannitol', a new weapon with which to fight Ciguatera fish poisoning, the most common form of fish poisoning in the region. The substance of the cure is described, as are the symptoms of fish poisoning. The breakthrough first appeared in a *New York Times* article on 13 May.

217 **Health and social aspects of child development for nurses, teachers and parents.**
Maria L. Barker. Road Town, Tortola: Ministry of Health, Pan-American World Organization, World Health Organization, 1979. 39p.
In the summary report of a workshop held on 28-29 November and sponsored by the Medical and Health Department of the British Virgin Islands, ideas are conveyed for incorporating all three departments when designing programmes and curricula relating to the three crucial stages of child development.

218 **Health, Education and Welfare sponsors Nutrition Workshop.**
*Island Sun*, vol. 29, no. 1516 (18 May 1991), p. 7.
A two-day workshop to upgrade and introduce new knowledge and skills for promoting good nutrition was held in the British Virgin Islands on 14-15 May 1991. According to the report, the workshop was held under the auspices of the Ministry of Health, Education and Welfare and the Pan-American Health Organization (PAHO). Copies of the report are available from the Ministry of Health, Road Town, Tortola, British Virgin Islands.

219  **The historical context of medical practice in the British Virgin Islands.**
Michael O'Neal.  *Caribbean Perspectives* (submitted for publication
1985). 24p. bibliog.
An excellent bibliographical paper which surveys early literature on aspects of medical
care in the British Caribbean plantation society. The British Virgin Islands is especially
treated under the heading 'Medical care in the British Virgin Islands: an historical
review', which commences with biographical vignettes of two Virgin Islands physicians
of the plantation era, John Coakley Lettsome and William Thornton. The conclusion
sums up the progress made in the public health sector over the years: 'the crude death
rate of 17.2 per thousand in 1911 had declined to 8.6 in 1964' . . . and there is 'roughly
one physician per 1000 persons'. Part of the paper was presented at the sixth annual
British Virgin Islands Medical Conference in February 1984. Although at the time of
going to press we have not discovered whether it was published in the journal to which
it was submitted, it is an important work already quoted in at least two published texts.
Further information may be obtained from PO Box 35, Road Town, Tortola, British
Virgin Islands. (The periodical was originally known as the *Journal of the College of
the Virgin Islands*.)

220  **Nurses create five year plan.**
John Clark.  *British Virgin Island Beacon*, vol. 6, no. 25 (30 Nov.
1989), p. 1.
Among the many needs of the nursing profession in the Islands, which surfaced as the
major concerns during a recent workshop to formulate a five-year development plan, is
the need for 'improved recruitment and training, including adaptation to new
technology'. The plan is available from Rita Georges, Chief Nursing Officer, Road
Town, Tortola, British Virgin Islands.

221  **Nurses focus on mental health.**
*Island Sun*, vol. 29, no. 1615 (18 May 1991), p. 19, 30.
A long historical account of the work of the Mental Health Association from its
initiation in 1972 is given in this report. There is special treatment celebrating Nurses
Week with its theme of 'Mental health nurses in action'. It lists the founding members
of the executive, with Rita Frett Georges, as founder; the goals of the Association;
notable achievements; various seminars held; and a new challenging programme for
the 1990s. Notable achievements of the Association's efforts include: the establishment
of a Mental Health Centre; and a new Mental Health Ordinance which was passed in
1985 to replace outdated legislation. There are photographs of the founding executive
and of the 1991 staff.

222  **Peebles Hospital golden jubilee magazine.**
Rita Georges (chairman magazine committee), foreword by Norwell
Harrigan.  Road Town, Tortola: British Virgin Islands Nurses
Association, 44p.
Marks a significant milestone in medical care in the islands. It sets out the history of
the hospital from 1926 to 1976, and pays tribute to early doctors and nurses with
photographs, lists and profiles. Significant articles come from a cross-section of the
community and include: 'Making bricks without straw' by J.R. O'Neal; 'Recollections'
by Adina Donovan; 'Nurse Wheatley looks back' by Jennie Wheatley; 'A fond look
back' by Eileen Parsons; 'Because you gave and cared' by Esmie Downing;
'Environmental health services' by Aubrey George; 'Sanitation' by Stanford Connor;

'Mental health' by Rita Georges; 'Development and growth' by Geraldine Norman; 'Peebles today' by Robin Tattersall and Carlos Downing; 'Renovation and extension' by Dr H.P. Watson, the then Chief Medical Officer. It is appropriately designed by Virgin Islands Publishing Company with a front-cover illustration showing the proposed Peebles Hospital by architect Ira Smith, while the back-cover illustration by Rueben Vanterpool shows how the original Cottage Hospital looked. On pages 8 and 10 there are elaborate plans for an extended and modernized hospital built around the existing building.

223 **Perceptions of mental illness in the Anglophone Caribbean.**
Michael O'Neal.   In: *Papers presented at a colloquium on mind, consciousness and sensibilities in Caribbean cultures*.   Pittsburgh: University of Pittsburgh, May 1985. 23p.
The author presents some anthropological perspectives on selected issues.

224 **Plastic surgeons hold international symposium in Tortola.**
Trenton Field.   *Island Sun*, vol. 29, no. 1600 (2 Feb. 1991), p. 1, 2.
Field provides information on the fifth annual British Virgin Islands workshop in plastic surgery. The doctors attending from USA, Barbados, UK, Sweden, Peru, the Netherlands and the British Virgin Islands discussed problems and exchanged information about complications and innovations in plastic surgery in relation to skin tumours and hand, trauma and aesthetic surgery. The workshop was sponsored by Butterworth Hospital Department of Continuing Medical Education and Providence Hospital Cranio-Facial Plastic and Reconstructive Surgery Centre, and its goal was to enhance the continuing medical education of surgeons in multiple plastic surgery disciplines. Papers may be obtained from Dr Ralph Blocksma, Road Town, Tortola, British Virgin Islands.

225 **Strategy to promote successful breastfeeding in the British Virgin Islands.**
St. Augustine, Trinidad: World Health Organization, Pan-American Health Organization, Caribbean Food and Nutrition Institute, [n.d.]. 19p.
Deals with the advantages of breastfeeding, and develops a programme for integration in the health services and health education.

# Virgin Islands, US

226 **Cultural aspects of delusion: a psychiatric study of the Virgin Islands.**
Edwin Alexander Weinstein, foreword by David McK. Rioch.   New York: Free Press of Glencoe, 1962. 215p. map. bibliog.
This monograph presents a combined psychiatric and anthropological approach to the study of delusions, hallucinations and other communications of patients in psychotic states. The analysis of symbolic behaviour extends into the area of psychotic

communication, earlier research of the author and a colleague – 'the symbolic behaviour of patients with brain injury'. There are relevant chapters on island cultural groups; institutional sources of identity; parent–child relationships; language; religion and symbolic aspects of death; obeah and witchcraft; minorities. The work is based on two-and-a-half years of living and working in the United States Virgin Islands and also includes field visits once a week to British Tortola. One measure of the importance of this work is revealed in the demonstration of a practical method for improving communication between the therapeutic staff and the patients.

227 **Illustrious past, challenging future: historical prospective of nursing in the United States Virgin Islands.**
Edited by Ilva F. Benjamin, Evelyn I. Price.   St. Thomas: Virgin Islands Nurses' Association, 1976. 23p.
Although brief, this salute traces two hundred years of nursing in the islands. It is vividly illustrated.

228 **Virgin Islands territorial adolescent pregnancy and prevention services programme.**
Charlotte Amalie, St. Thomas: Department of Health, 1980. [n.p.].
Seen as a significant tool for family planning, this document outlines the large scale of the problem of teenage pregnancy and offers a programme of services which should be made available to young people in the three-island territory.

# Women's Affairs

## General

**229  Caribbean women: their history and habits.**
G.K. Osei.   London: African Publication Society, 1979. 191p. bibliog.
Through this chronicle of roles and moods which are rooted in the past and living history of the region, the author shows how the Caribbean woman has taken her place alongside the man in building a Caribbean society and nation. It is an 'epic [of the] suffering and glorious achievement of Caribbean women'. References to the weed woman, also known as the 'bush medicine woman', and to Queen Mary – one of the most prominent persons involved in the 'Fireburn' revolt of St. Croix – are made on pages 113 and 148.

**230  Selected bibliography of materials and resources on women in the Caribbean available at WAND's research and documentation centre.**
Diane Innis.   Bridgetown, Barbardos: University of the West Indies, WAND, 1988. 97p.
An excellent tool for locating teaching aids, organizations and human resources on women's affairs in the Caribbean.

## Virgin Islands, UK

**231  Women and politics.**
*Island Sun* (4 Aug. 1990), p. 3.
In this issue, the editorial discusses how women in the British Virgin Islands relate to politics.

232 **Women taking a development role.**
Kenneth Clark. *British Virgin Island Beacon*, vol. 5, no. 18 (13 Oct. 1988) p. 1, 9.
Clark reports on a seminar with the theme 'Women's roles', sponsored by the British Virgin Islands Health Department, the Pan-American Health Organization, the World Health Organization and the Canadian International Development Agency. The report emphasizes the contribution that women have already made to community development and calls on women to recognize their extended role in further developing the nation. Copies of the proceedings may be obtained from: The Medical And Health Department, Road Town, Tortola, British Virgin Islands.

**British Virgin Islands: territorial report for the year 1987.**
*See* item no. 9.

**The Abolition Act 1833.**
*See* item no. 139.

# Virgin Islands, US

233 **Women of accomplishment.**
Charlotte Amalie, St. Thomas: Virgin Islands Federation of Business and Professional Women's Clubs, 1977. 66p.
A corporate and illustrative achievement, the work records the biographies, struggles and successes of some of the islands' remarkable women.

# Human Rights

234 **British Virgin Islands.**
Special Committee on the situation with regard to the implementation of the declaration on the granting of the independence to colonial countries and peoples. New York: UN General Assembly, 1981. 17p.
Prepared by the secretariat of the UN General Assembly, this paper gives a candid description of constitutional and political developments, economic activity, social and educational conditions in the islands.

235 **Human Rights covenants.**
*Island Sun*, no. 1570 (23 June 1990), p. 1.
A brief but important report on the tabling of two international covenants on human rights (the International Covenant on Economic, Social and Cultural Rights, and the one on Civil and Political Rights). Both covenants were ratified by the British Virgin Islands government on 20 June 1990.

**America's Virgin Islands: a history of human rights and wrongs.**
*See* item no. 145.

**The history of the legislature of the United States Virgin Islands.**
*See* item no. 248.

# Politics

## General

236 **Caribbean and world politics: cross currents and cleavages.**
Edited by Jorge Heine, Leslie Manigat. New York: Holmes and
Meier, 1988. 385p. bibliog.

This comprehensive effort, the work of several contributors, is divided into four major
sections: 'Geopolitics and international political economy' by Leslie Manigat, Carl
Stone, Mirlande Manigat and Trevor Farrell; 'Caribbean foreign policies: cases and
courses' by Vaughan Lewis, Paul Ashley and Jean Crusol; 'The role of some regional
middle powers' by Kari Levitt, Fernando Cepeda and Mirlande Manigat; and 'The
United States and the Caribbean' by Edward Gonzales, Robert Pastor and Anthony
Manigat. Additionally, there is an epilogue by Leslie Manigat and a bibliographical
guide by Jorge Heine. There are several references to both groups of Virgin Islands,
but greater coverage is given to the United States Virgin Islands. On page 11,
reference is made to 'the appointment of Terrance Todman, a Virgin Islander, as
Assistant Secretary of State for Inter American Affairs and hearings in the House of
Representatives, on the state of United States Caribbean relations, signalled a new
awareness of the need to focus more closely on the region'. Canadian exports and
imports to and from the United States Virgin Islands, the type of economy, the
standard of living and its major trading partners, are mentioned on pages 231-3.
References to the British Virgin Islands appear in various tables illustrating the type of
government, the Gross National Product (GNP) per capita, life expectancy, and
unemployment.

237 **The negro in the Caribbean.**
Eric Williams. Washington, DC: Associates in Negro Folk Education,
1942. 119p. bibliog.

This analysis sets the West Indies in its historical past and presents problems in a
challenging and constructive interpretation, looking towards the future. Although now
dated, the issues are still relevant in terms of solving problems which will lead to

constructive enlargement of Western democracy. (A paperback edition was published in 1976.)

238 **Party politics in the West Indies.**
Edited by C.L.R. James, foreword by R.M. Walters.    [n.p.]: Imprint Caribbean, 1984. 184p.

First published in 1962 merely 'as a public statement' by a distinguished Caribbean writer on the local political scene. James's famous line, 'the people know that all is not well, that there are realities which all the talk does not touch', is an example of what makes this author 'the creative political theorist', so highly acclaimed on the international scene.

239 **Seize the time: towards the Organisation of Eastern Caribbean States (OECS) Political Union.**
William G. Demas.    St. Michael, Barbados: Caribbean Development Bank, 1987. 57p.

Based on an address on political unity in the Eastern Caribbean, the President of the Caribbean Development Bank states the case for wider political union in the West Indies. He answers such questions as: why is it necessary to start with the OECS? and which form of political unity should it take? This has some force for the British Virgin Islands which became a member of the OECS in 1984.

# Virgin Islands, UK

240 **Address delivered on the occasion of the naming of the government administration building in Anegada in honour of politician Theodolph Faulkner.**
Pearl I. Varlack.    *Island Sun*, vol. 29, no. 1611 (20 April 1991), p. 12, 14.

The address speaks of the late Theodolph Faulkner as an enterprising community man, a beloved father and as the politician who 'struck the match that was the beginning of the end of highhandedness . . . providing that leaven which led to a certain level of self-government in these islands'. Pearl Varlack is Professor of Education at the University of the Virgin Islands of the United States.

241 **Networks, groups and local level politics in an Afro-Caribbean community.**
Robert Dirks.    PhD thesis, Case Western Reserve University, 1971. 297p. bibliog. maps.

By drawing contrasts between personal networks and corporate groups, the work indicates how these two variants provide a framework of political alternatives in the arena of intra-community competition for land. It suggests that the continual efforts to organize public support with respect to land claims provide the community with a kind of procession order. It further proposes that the order is generated by an attempt to maintain a relatively secure niche as insurance against failure in a marginal society.

242 **Memoirs of H.R. Penn.**
Howard Reynold Penn, foreword by Governor J.M.A. Herdman, introduction by J.R. O'Neal. Road Town, Tortola: The author, 1991. 72p.
A personal account of the history and politics of the British Virgin Islands in the twentieth century, from one of the territory's most distinguished sons and politicians. The memoirs speak of his struggles as a politician to secure the dignity of his countrymen and the territory's prosperous future. They also capture the colourful history of trade, constitutional changes, banking and the physical construction of the territory.

243 **Power by accident: the making of the Chief Minister.**
Norwell Harrigan. *Island Sun*, vol. 28, no. 1550 (24 March 1990), p. 15. (As We See Ourselves series).
The beginning of a five-part series which examines the political evolution in the British Virgin Islands from 1774 onwards. This first part entitled 'The waiting years', gives a historical synopsis up to 1967. The other parts are: 'Problems of leadership', vol. 28, no. 1552 (31 March 1990), p. 6, 15; 'Shadows of Westminister', vol. 28, no. 1554 (7 April 1990), p. 15.; 'Changing the image', vol. 28, no. 1555 (14 April 1990) p. 3; 'The next step', vol. 28, no. 1556 (21 April 1990), p. 23. This last part discusses four possibilities for improving the machinery for selecting a chief minister. It concludes with a suggestion for the formulation of a Citizens' Committee to discuss futher details and to sponsor a conference on constitutional change. It is an objective and interesting study of the political scene in a mini-state.

244 **The programme for the 1990s and a better tomorrow.**
Virgin Islands Party. *Island Sun* (20 Oct. 1990), p. 18-19.
This is the political manifesto of the Virgin Islands Party (VIP). It details the party's plans for economic goals, social services, public works, constitution, legislators' pension, and law and order. A precise list of priorities for the 1990s is also recorded.

245 **Report of the general elections, 1990.**
Eugenie Todman-Smith. Road Town, Tortola: British Virgin Islands Government, 1991. 35p.
Tabling its contents under eight headings – introduction, recommendations, administration of the election process, the Elections (Amendment) Act 1990, communication, election offences, nomination of candidates, and polling day – this is an outstanding report. It records the major differences between the 1990 election and those in the past, and credits the new Election (Amendment) Act passed on 17 September 1990, with bringing them about. There are twenty-eight recommendations, one of which is that telephones should be installed at all polling stations. Appendixes include lists of election officers, nominated candidates, polling stations, statistical returns for each electoral district, and of successful candidates.

246  **Roll of Legislative Council menbers.**
H.R. Penn, Janice Nibbs, Verna Penn Moll.  *Virgin Islands Historical Documents*, vol. 1, no. 4 (Oct.-Dec. 1984), p. 5-6.

Tastefully designed on the centre pages, this scroll lists Legislative Council members of the British Virgin Islands government, from 1950 to 1983. Compiled from Legislative Council minutes, it names elected members, nominated members and official members. It makes a handy reference work.

**Stateman's year book, 1990-91.**
*See* item no. 6.

**British Virgin Islands: territorial report for the year 1987.**
*See* item no. 9.

**Geopolitics of the Caribbean: ministates in a wider world.**
*See* item no. 19.

**A concise history of the Virgin Islands.**
*See* item no. 120.

**The Virgin Islands story.**
*See* item no. 126.

**Development, immigration and politics in a pre-industrial society . . .**
*See* item no. 200.

**Women and politics.**
*See* item no. 231.

**Women taking a development role.**
*See* item no. 232.

# Virgin Islands, US

247  **Changing patterns of local reaction to the United States acquisition of the Virgin Islands.**
Isaac Dookhan.  *Caribbean Studies*, vol. 15, no. 1 (April 1975), p. 50-72. bibliog.

Detailed and articulate, this article provides a substantial account of the metamorphosis in attitudes in some sectors of a community which once accepted the 'stars and stripes' without question.

248    **The history of the legislature of the United States Virgin Islands.**
John Collins.    Charlotte Amalie, St. Thomas: The legislature, 1983.
92p.
A concise history of the legislature, which also embodies a chapter on the political
history by former governor Ralph M. Paiewonsky (p. 39). Photographs of early
legislators, with a special sequence of women legislators, accompany the text.

249    **Virgin Islands, America's Caribbean outpost: the evolution of self
government.**
Edited by J. Bough, Roy C. Macridis.    Wakefield, Massachusetts:
Walter F. Williams, 1970. 232p.
This important work is based on the proceedings of a conference on the evolving status
of the Virgin Islands which was held in St. Thomas from 30 March to 1 April 1968. It is
set out in three sections: basic documents; papers; and political attitudes in the Virgin
Islands.

250    **Virgin Islands election laws.**
United States Government.    New York: Butterworth Legal
Publications, 1988. 200p.
A useful document which brings together the laws that govern the election process in
the United States Virgin Islands.

**Statesman's year book, 1990-91.**
*See* item no. 6.

**The United States Virgin Islands.**
*See* item no. 136.

**Women of accomplishment.**
*See* item no. 233.

**Virgin Islands of the United States: Blue Book.**
*See* item no. 601.

# Foreign Affairs

## Inter-Virgin Islands

251 **British Virgin Islands/United States Virgin Islands to convene Inter-Virgin Islands Conference.**
British Virgin Islands/United States Virgin Islands Governments.
*News Release*, no. 272R/90 (25 Oct. 1990), 2p.
Issued jointly by the governments of the British and United States Virgin Islands, the release states that the governments will reconvene the Inter-Virgin Islands Conference between the two territories on BVI-USVI Friendship Day scheduled for 27 October 1990. Originally established as a forum to discuss socio-economic issues including fishing, immigration, labour, health care, trade and transportation, between the two governments, the Conference last met in 1965. The document further states that the reactivation of the Conference will begin with the signing of a new Memorandum of Understanding during ceremonies at Government House in the United States Virgin Islands during Friendship Day.

252 **The Inter-Virgin Islands Conference: a study of a Microstate International Organization.**
Norwell Harrigan.   Gainesville, Florida: Centre for Latin American Studies, University of Florida and University Presses of Florida for the Caribbean Research Institute, College of the Virgin Islands, [n.d.].
88p. bibliog.
A study which reviews the original institutional framework whereby both groups of Virgin Islands 'would seek a working relationship'. It analyses the economic forces which compelled those two non-sovereign territories to structure the conference; it describes the machinery and processes of the conference; and forecasts the prospects for future co-operation along similar lines. There are useful appendixes including the 'Joint memorandum establishing the Inter-Virgin Islands Conference'. The work is a

significant one in the series of microstate studies being sponsored by the Caribbean Research Institute.

253  **Inter-Virgin Islands Conference.**
Lavity Stoutt.   Road Town, Tortola: Chief Minister's Office, 1990. 4p.

In his address on the occasion of the second Inter-Virgin Islands Conference, the Honourable Lavity Stoutt (Chief Minister of the British Virgin Islands) briefly outlined the history (from 1951) and the functions of the Conference. He emphasized old and new issues which the conference must tackle, noting that both territories want the same things: '. . . clean air, clean seas and clean land. A joint environmental policy formulated by the Conference and implemented by our Governments can give the people what they want'.

254  **Virgin Islands inter-relationships programme.**
Norwell Harrigan.   St. Thomas: Caribbean Research Institute, 1971.
7p.

Submitted on 31 August 1971, this final report outlines a plan of action that would bring both groups – the British and United States Virgin Islands – together more frequently for meetings and activities.

# International relations

255  **Heads of Government of Commonwealth western hemisphere countries.**
*Caribbean Monthly Bulletin*, vol. 17, nos 3-4 (March-April 1983), p. 5.

Communiqué of a meeting held on 20-21 February at which the British Virgin Islands was represented. The meeting was held at St. Lucia and twenty-three points were raised by the various heads of government. The major focus was on relations in terms of trade, development assistance, investment, tourism, and political developments in the hemisphere. As regards the disposition of outside forces to intervene, the communiqué states that the meeting reasserted the view that each state must be allowed to pursue its own political, economic and social development free from all forms of external interference, coercion, intimidation and pressure.

256  **Nineteen seventy seven: the Queen's silver jubilee.**
Road Town, Tortola: British Virgin Islands Government, 1977. 39p.
map.

Published to mark the visit of Her Majesty the Queen and His Royal Highness Prince Philip to the British Virgin Islands on 26 October 1977, during the Queen's silver jubilee year, this little booklet not only contains the itinerary of the royal visit, but also various aspects of the territory's history, highlighting the British connection and the islands' development. There are several illustrations of places of interest en route and the centre pages carry the map and track of H.M. Yacht *Britannia* on 26 October. The work was researched and designed by V.E. Penn.

257 **Proposed United Kingdom – United States Treaty endorsed by British Virgin Islands parliament.**
Trenton Field. *Island Sun*, no. 1580 (8 Sept. 1990), p. 1.
The Mutual Legal Assistance (USA) Act 1990 was, according to Field, passed at a recent sitting of the British Virgin Islands Legislative Council, but not without sceptical comments from some members of the meeting. The overall aim of passing the Act is 'to discourage criminals seeking the territory as a place of refuge'.

258 **Statement on acceptance of the British and United States Virgin Islands to the United Nations Economic Commission for Latin America (ECLA).**
C.B. Romney. *Caribbean Monthly Bulletin*, vol. 18. nos 4-6 (April-June 1984), p. 92-4.
Four prime objectives are presented in the document: to improve the quality of life for all citizens through the pursuit of full employment objectives; to control the development and exploitation of our natural resources for the benefit of the indigenous population; to provide opportunities for native investment through the encouragement of individual effort and joint ventures between local and foreign investors; and to maintain a stable, peaceful and harmonious society wherein all of the above may be safely and quietly achieved.

259 **The United States in the Caribbean.**
Isaac Dookhan. London: Collins, 108p. maps. bibliog.
This is one of a series in which a number of Caribbean historians have each chosen a theme to explore in depth. This theme – 'the United States in the Caribbean' – is well presented with pictures and maps to heighten readers' concentration. It is in the History topics listing for the Caribbean Examinations series. Both economic and political ties are expounded.

**Discover.**
*See* item no. 10.

**Geopolitics of the Caribbean: ministates in a wider world.**
*See* item no. 19.

**A history of the British Virgin Islands, 1672 to 1970.**
*See* item no. 122.

# Virgin Islands, US

260 **American Revolution's second front: places and persons involved in the Danish West Indies and some other West Indian Islands.**
Florence Lewisohn.   Charlotte Amalie, St. Thomas: Caribbean Research Institute in association with the American Revolution Bicentennial Commission, 1976. 66p. bibliog.
A study of the naval and diplomatic action which swirled in and around the Danish West Indies, the British Virgin Islands and nearby Leeward Islands during the revolution. It includes the part played by agents and spies; lessons in ingenuity, co-operation and survival among many nationalities neutral or otherwise, as the British swept the seas on this second front.

261 **The transition from the Danish colony to American territory, 1865-1917.**
Staff of Enid Baa Public Library and Archives (researched by Helen King).   Charlotte Amalie, St. Thomas: Bureau of Libraries and Museums, 1975. 18p.
An in-depth chronology of the transfer of the Danish West Indies which attempts to illustrate the complexities of diplomatic negotiations and the broad scope of international factors affecting negotiations. Although the illustrations are not crisp, they are of historical importance; they include, for example, one by Clare E. Taylor showing St. Thomians assembled to witness the transfer ceremony.

262 **The United States Virgin Islands: 'foreign' operations in a United States possession.**
Edward E. Thomas.   Englewood Cliffs, New Jersey: Prentice-Hall, 1984. p. 8741-59. (Reprinted from: *United States taxation of internal operations service*).
This reprint examines the fine print of the code and 'mirror theory' and shows how to get an adequate return on an investment without undue tax exposure.

263 **What so proudly we hail.**
Florence Lewisohn.   Charlotte Amalie, St. Thomas: American Revolution Bicentennial Commission, 1975. 51p. bibliog.
Three studies of island events relating to the American Revolution: How the Danish islands aided the rebels with cautious support and recognition of their flags; How Alexander Hamilton grew up on St. Croix; and How the Dutch ran a huge supply centre for rebel privateers.

**A history of the Virgin Islands of the United States.**
*See* item no. 130.

**In Danish times.**
*See* item no. 131.

# Constitution and Legal System

## Virgin Islands, UK

264 **British Virgin Islands constitution.**
*British Virgin Islands Historical Documents*, vol. 2. no. 1 (March-April 1985), p. 6-10.
Contains the main sections – from one to twelve – of the text of the British Virgin Islands constitution; and deals with the appointment and functions of the Governor and Deputy Governor. In addition, the constitution lists the powers of the Governor as follows: to dispose of land; to constitute offices and make appointments; powers of pardon; and the establishment of the Mercy Advisory Committee. The excerpt was taken from: The Virgin Islands Constitution Order, 1976, laid before Parliament 23 December 1976, coming into operation 1 June 1977; amended 1979, 1982 (Statutory Instruments, 1976, no. 2145; Caribbean & North Atlantic Territories).

265 **The growth of the operation of the judicial system of the British Virgin Islands.**
McWelling Todman. *Island Sun* (23 June 1977), p. 9, 13.
An enlightening overview of the judicial system in the British Virgin Islands, from the disgraceful courts of the colonists to today, when 'the British Virgin Islands can boast one lawyer to every 750 of the population – a ratio equalled perhaps by only Israel and the United States'.

266 **Report of the British Virgin Islands constitutional conference.**
M. Proudfoot. London: HMSO for British Virgin Islands Government, 1966. 69p.
Based on the proceedings of the specially commissioned constitutional conference of 1965, this report outlines the various forms of government the country had experienced and suggests several alternatives. It is the backbone on which the present constitution

hangs. The appendixes include a list of participants and their contributions to the conference.

267 **British Virgin Islands consolidated index of statutes and subsidiary legislation to 1st January, 1989.**
Faculty of Law Library, University of the West Indies. [n.p.], Florida: Gaunt, 1989. 71p.
An index of laws of the territory of the British Virgin Islands, arranged by title and reference number. It includes laws, statutes and statutory instruments passed from 31 October 1985 to 1988.

268 **British Virgin Islands laws, 7 vols.**
Edited by Cecil Lewis. London: British Virgin Islands Government, 1961, rev. ed.
Replaces the 18th-century edition although there are still some outdated laws on the books. There is a separate index.

**New insurance legislation.**
*See* item no. 316.

**Labour Code Ordinance, 1975.**
*See* item no. 380.

**British Virgin Islands: harmonization of environmental legislation – report and draft legislation for coastal conservation.**
*See* item no. 420.

**British Virgin Islands: harmonization of environmental legislation – report and draft legislation on protected areas and wildlife conservation.**
*See* item no. 421.

# Virgin Islands, US

269 **The Virgin Islands Code.**
Washington, DC: Department of the Interior, 1957. 5 vols.
The Code became effective on 1 September 1957. It contains the general and permanent laws in force in the United States Virgin Islands. A cumulated pocket supplement to the laws was issued in 1964 with 193 pages, and in 1967 another supplement was issued with 16 pages.

**Constitution and Legal System.** Virgin Islands, US

**Brief history of the Virgin Islands.**
*See* item no. 127.

**St. Croix at the 20th century: a chapter in its history.**
*See* item no. 132.

**Virgin Islands corporation laws.**
*See* item no. 339.

# Administration and Local Government

## Virgin Islands, UK

**270  British Virgin Islands Public Service Staff List.**
Deputy Governor's Office.    Road Town, Tortola: British Virgin
Islands Government, 1987. 58p.

Published periodically, this edition is revised up to April 1987. It lists all government
employees showing the departmental structure of staff and salary scales. Committees
and responsibilities are defined and appointments and benefits explained.

**271  General orders for the Public Service of the British Virgin Islands.**
Deputy Governor's Office.    Road Town, Tortola: British Virgin
Islands Government, 1971. 54p.

Sets out the terms and conditions of employment in the Civil Service. Sections deal in
detail with recruitment and appointment, conduct, staff structure and qualifications,
salaries and allowances, hours, leave, pensions and other benefits. The handbook is
amended periodically to include changes in policy, for example, the raising of the age
limit whereby female employees may be retained in the service. The orders were
revised it 1982.

**272  Review of a top management workshop.**
Ministers, permanent secretaries and heads of departments.    Road
Town, Tortola: Establishment Department, Government of the
British Virgin Islands, Department of the Government of the
University of the West Indies and the Canadian International
Development Agency, 1985. 21p.

Both the background and purpose of the workshop which the political directorate and
civil service managers attended are recorded in this report. It was convened to review
the first workshop held in May 1983. Ten recommendations are listed and include 'the
development of relevant procedural manuals in the Public Sector'.

273 **Speech from the throne.**
J.M.A. Herdman.   Road Town, Tortola: British Virgin Islands
Government, 1990. 7p.

A summary of the Government's programme for the year 1991. Issued annually and
presented by the Governor of the territory, this publication is a quick index to the
Government's intentions and policies affecting all sectors. This one was presented at
the formal opening of the twelfth Legislative Council on Friday, 7 December 1990.

# Virgin Islands, US

274 **The Virgin Islands: a citizens' handbook.**
St. Thomas: League of Women Voters of the Virgin Islands, 1971. 43p.

The politics and government of the territory are explained in layman's language.

275 **The Virgin Islands of the United States.**
Waldo Evans.   Washington, DC: United States Government Printing
Office, 1928. 102p.

A general report on the islands by the then Governor. It provides a first-hand account
of all aspects of the administration and development of the islands in the 19th century,
and up to the beginning of the second decade of their acquisition by America from
Denmark. Current reports are also available for comparative studies on the islands'
progress.

**Government Information Service Bulletin.**
*See* item no. 580.

**Virgin Islands government directory.**
*See* item no. 600.

**Virgin Islands of the United States: Blue Book.**
*See* item no. 601.

# Statistics

## General

276  **Statistical survey of the Virgin Islands.**
*Europa yearbook*, vol. 2 (1990), p. 2748-51, 2882-4.
Statistical records of areas and population, agriculture, industry, finance, external trade, transport, education, constitution, political organizations, the judicial system, religion, the press, radio and television, trade and industry. The work is an authoritative source for up-to-date figures and information.

277  **Statistical yearbook.**
Paris: UNESCO, 1990. (var. pag.).
The world's statistics are tabulated under headings such as education, literacy, culture and communication, libraries, and science and technology. The Virgin Islands are represented in most areas; the British Virgin Islands country number is 61 and that of the United States Virgin Islands is 91.

## Virgin Islands, UK

278  **British Virgin Islands tourism review.**
Road Rown, Tortola: Development Planning Office, 1990. 61p.
Mainly statistics, this report reviews the tourist trade for the year 1989. There are statistics on tourism arrivals, departures, accommodation, means of transport, and the various classes of visitors.

279 **Banking statistics.**
Road Town, Tortola: Ministry of Finance, Development Planning Unit, 1987. 33p.
Appearing annually, this is a vital source of current information on commercial banking activity in the British Virgin Islands. A special appendix surveys the financial operations and activities of the Government and the Social Security Board. The series first appeared in 1975.

280 **Economic statistics.**
Pierre Encontre. *British Virgin Island Beacon*, vol. 5, no. 40 (30 March 1989), p. 1, 7.
United Nations economic adviser, Encontre – who works in the British Virgin Islands – produces various statistics relating to imports and exports, trade balances, visitors, and investments for the British Virgin Islands and the United States Virgin Islands. The report, drawn up for the *Beacon*, concludes that the British Virgin Islands contribute more to the economy of the United States Virgin Islands than the latter does to the former.

281 **Tourism in the British Virgin Islands 1986: a statistical analysis.**
Road Town, Tortola: Ministry of Finance, Development Planning Unit, 1987. 51p.
The report provides statistical data for the previous year; it also has an historical appendix covering the previous twelve years and showing visitor arrivals, accommodation, and expenditure estimates. The series, of which this is number thirteen, provides an important basis for analysing the growth and structural variation of the British Virgin Islands tourism sector.

282 **The use of input–output analysis for income and employment projections.**
A. Bottomley. *Caribbean Studies*, vol. 18, nos 3, 4 (1978), p. 157-74.
Although this article is now dated, the principles employed for analysing statistics are still relevant to similar studies. The British Virgin Islands was used in this case.

283 **Vital statistics report, no. 3.**
Road Town, Tortola: Ministry of Finance, Development Planning Unit, Statistics Office, 1987. 65p.
This is the third in a series of vital statistics reports, covering population, births, deaths, marriages, divorces, and health-related statistics such as live births, diseases, teenage pregnancies, etc.

**The Commonwealth year book, 1990.**
*See* item no. 4.

**Statesman's year book, 1990-91.**
*See* item no. 6.

**British Virgin Islands: territorial report for the year 1987.**
*See* item no. 9.

**The Virgins: a descriptive and historical profile.**
*See* item no. 25.

**Labour Department: report for the year 1987.**
*See* item no. 381.

**1980-1991 census of the Commonwealth Caribbean: British Virgin Islands, volume one.**
*See* item no. 157.

**United Nations Conference on Trade and Development.**
*See* item no. 310.

# Virgin Islands, US

284 **Lists of vital statistics.**
Harvey Chipkin, Bernice Carton. *Meetings and Conventions*, vol. 22 (April 1987), p. 10-17.
In this guide to Puerto Rico, United States Virgin Islands, Jamaica and the Bahamas, there are important figures on population, employment, and the GNP relating to the United States Virgin Islands.

**Caribbean ethnicity revisited.**
*See* item no. 158.

**A profile of Frederiksted, St. Croix, United States Virgin Islands.**
*See* item no. 291.

# Economy and Investment

## Virgin Islands, UK

285  **Anegada – feudal development in the twentieth century.**
Pearl Varlack, Norwell Harrigan.  *Caribbean Quarterly*, vol. 17, no. 1
(March 1971), p. 5-15. bibliog.

A discussion of the early history and economic stagnation of Anegada and the attempt
of the Development Corporation to 'put the island on the road to progress'. The terms
of the lease (including obligations and privileges) between the Government and the
Corporation are recorded, as is the full text of an opposing resolution (with all the
preamble) which was introduced in the Legislative Council. The aftermath of the
onslaught was the announcement of the appointment of a Commission of Enquiry with
specific terms of reference: 'To examine the Anegada Agreement . . . in the light of
the interests of the people of the British Virgin Islands, the inhabitants of Anegada,
the parties of the agreement and all other persons or corporations who have invested in
the development of Anegada . . .' and to report on certain matters and make
recommendations on the future development of Anegada in general, including whether
a new development concept should be developed for the island. The paper raises a
number of questions and the authors conclude that 'regardless of the findings of the
Commission, this is a matter for political determination. And the people of the British
Virgin Islands appear bent on making the decision'.

286  **Better prospects for the British Virgin Islands.**
McWelling Todman.  *Financial Times* (21 May 1971), p. 29.

Lawyer Todman skilfully reviews past economic performance and scans the horizon for
new prospects.

287  **British Virgin Islands: a report.**
Stewart Fleming.  *Financial Times* (29 Sept. 1976), p. 27-9.

Fleming outlines the subsistence economy and constitutional moves which would give
the islands a greater degree of self-determination.

288   **The national consultation on human resource development planning.**
Salasan Associates, Inc.   Road Town, Tortola: Chief Minister's Office,
CTAP, 1987. [n.p.].
This records the results of a workshop held for senior government and business leaders
on resource development planning. The workshop examined locally perceived trends in
economic change in order to assist in assessing the human resource needs of the
country.

289   **Social and economic review no. 3.**
Development Planning Unit, foreword by Otto O'Neal.   Road Town,
Tortola: Chief Minister's Office, British Virgin Islands Government,
1988. 174p.
Detailed and massive, this work interprets the state of the territory's social and
economic performance with text and figures. Section one gives an overview of
international, Latin American, Caribbean and domestic developments. On the
domestic scene, one of the major policy decisons was 'to maximize revenue collections
without changing the tax base'. Section two deals with the macroeconomy and includes
the gross domestic product (GDP), balance of payments, external trade, inflation,
money and banking, fiscal policy and fiscal budget. Section three – sectoral
performance – analyses agriculture and fisheries, communications, construction and
installation, electricity and water, financial services, manufacturing, tourism and
transport, while section four deals with manpower and labour relations. Section five
treats human development and welfare, and section six provides lists of tables and
acronyms, and glossaries of economic, demographic and social terms. There are also
tables of statistics in their appropriate sections. All of these features make this an
important work of reference.

**British Virgin Islands: territorial report for the year 1987.**
*See* item no. 9.

**Regional tourism: economic planning, policy and research workshop.**
*See* item no. 75.

**Tourism management and environmental and development issues.**
*See* item no. 79.

**Why does the tourist dollar matter?: an introduction to the economics of
tourism in the British Virgin Islands.**
*See* item no. 80.

**Women taking a developmental role.**
*See* item no. 232.

**Development and land use programme for the British Virgin Islands.**
*See* item no. 356.

**Status of British Virgin Islands fisheries development.**
*See* item no. 370.

# Virgin Islands, US

290 **Planning a balanced economic development programme for small business in the United States Virgin Islands.**
Darwin Creque. Washington, DC: Department of Commerce, United States Virgin Islands Government, 1963.

Creque outlines a broad programme for the Virgin Islands Government and private enterprise, in order to stimulate economic development in the territory through industrial diversification. He gives the geographical, demographic and economic characteristics of the area as well as the objectives of the programme. Recommendations are made for achieving the objectives: 'promoting tourism and small manufactures that utilize local skills' and the establishing of a Central Economic Development Agency. An appendix lists statistics on external trade, population, minimum rates, income distribution, and power consumption.

291 **A profile of Frederiksted, St. Croix, United States Virgin Islands.**
S.B. Jones-Hendrickson. St. Thomas: Caribbean Research Institute, 1990. 191p. bibliog.

The author assesses the economy and politics of Frederiksted, the second largest town in St. Croix, and because it is 'the most underdeveloped area in the United States Virgin Islands', he makes suggestions for its revitalization. With accompanying graphs and many tables of statistics, the work is assembled in seven chapters covering such topics as: the history and socio-economic issues of Frederiksted; population; the labour force; housing; land and land values; health care delivery; business conditions; the future and revitalization. The author offers fourteen suggestions for revitalizing the town. All together, this is an important document with up-to-date references.

292 **The Virgin Islands Company and Corporation: the plan for economic rehabilitation in the Virgin Islands.**
Isaac Dookhan. *Journal of Caribbean History*, vol. 4 (May 1972), p. 54-76.

The article traces the economic development in the islands from 'effective poor house to the show piece of democracy in the western hemisphere'. It also shows how the Virgin Islands Company proved of great value in helping to ease the transition from agriculture to the tourism industry.

293 **The Virgin Islands economy.**
Jerome L. McElroy. Charlotte Amalie, St. Thomas: Planning Office, Office of the Governor, 1974. 128p.

Although this document is now quite dated, it is still useful for comparisons with the current situation. It describes past performance, future projections and planning alternatives.

**Women of accomplishment.**
*See* item no. 233.

**Essentials of farm financial management.**
*See* item no. 353.

**Land grant programmes in action.**
*See* item no. 358.

**Economic Review.**
*See* item no. 576.

**News and Views.**
*See* item no. 583.

# Finance, Banking and Currency

## General

294 **Caribbean Development Bank annual report.**
A.N. Robinson, Chairman.  St. Michael, Barbados: Caribbean
Development Bank, 1989. 177p.

The report of the regional financial institution, highlighting the activities of 1988. A review of the economic developments of the British Virgin Islands appears on pages 29-30.

295 **Sources and methods of estimating national income and product accounts for OECS member states.**
Hazel Corbin.  St. Johns, Antigua: OECS, Economic Affairs
Secretariat, 1985. 20p.

Provides a formula by which member states can calculate their national income rates.

296 **Survey of off-shore finance sectors in Caribbean dependent territories.**
Rodney Gallagher, Coopers and Lybrand.  London: HMSO, 1990.
156p.

Island by island, the report analyses each sector and provides useful guidelines for several of the Eastern Caribbean states. The British Virgin Islands section on pages 46-89 describes the role of the financial sector in the economy; administration and the Ministry of Finance; opportunities and contraints; the current legislation with propsals for change. A number of draft laws are included: draft insurance law, draft trust law, draft company mangament law, and guidelines for bank licensing. Given that the islands have become so active in the off-shore finance business, this document has appeared at a most opportune time.

# Virgin Islands, UK

297 **The beautiful and mysterious coins of the British Virgin Islands.**
Giorgio Migliavacca.   In: *British Virgin Islands Tourist Handbook,
1990*, edited by Vernon W. Pickering. Road Town, Tortola: Laurel,
1990, p. 69-81. bibliog.
An historical survey of local currency used in the British Virgin Islands from 1801 to
the present. The author uses pictures of 'cut money' from Pridmore's *Notes on
Colonial Coins* (published by Spink & Son Ltd in 1959) and from other sources to
illustrate the article appropriately.

298 **British Virgin Islands recurrent budget estimates of receipts and
expenditure: capital budget estimates of revenue and expenditure.**
Ministry of Finance.   Road Town, Tortola: British Virgin Islands
Government, 1989. 135p.
The actual figures and statements representing Government's plans and commitments
for administering services and projects during the year. It details and summarizes the
annual recurrent cost, and indicates assets and liabilities, revenue sources, expenditure
estimates, and figures for comparative years. Established posts and salary scales are
also presented.

299 **Budget address 1991.**
Lavity Stoutt.   Road Town, Tortola: British Virgin Islands Legislative
Council, 1991. 12p.
Delivered to the Legislative Council by the Minister of Finance (also the Chief
Minister) on 18 April 1991, this document addresses the fiscal goals and policies,
aspirations and challenges for the year 1991. Medium- and long-term goals are
condensed 'to transform these islands into a thriving and stable economy with state-of-
the-art communication technology . . . and to continue our programmes of performance'. The document notes eight major challenges that must be met: to accelerate
and broaden national training progammes; to upgrade essential public services; to
fully realize the country's potential to become one of the region's main service centres;
to promote and vigorously develop small business enterprises, cottage industries, and
artisans; to preserve the country's reputation as a first-rate centre for the conduct of
legitimate transnational business; to encourage high levels of domestic saving and
investment for national development; to use the instruments of public investment to
create opportunities for economic activity; and to restructure taxation policies which
will reduce tax burdens wherever possible. It details the out-turn of the provisional
1990 accounts and its beneficial impact, and lists thirteen capital development projects,
based on a three-year rolling plan. In the absence of a current development plan, this
document 'constitutes the most important single instrument of development policy'. It
is invaluable for programming development project activity in virtually every sector of
the economy; for allocating resources among competing wants; for determining
priorities; and for making choices.

300 **The dawn of a new era: British Virgin Islands emerges as a major financial service centre.**
*British Virgin Island Beacon*, vol. 6 no. 1 (8 June 1989), p. 16.
Assisted by tables and graphs, this five-column article analyses the success of the British Virgin Islands as a financial service centre. It concludes that the major contributing factors are: its political status as a UK dependent territory; political and economic stability; a highly developed legal system based on British common law; the ultra-modern corporate law (the International Business Companies Act) and the state-of-the-art telecommunication system.

301 **Income tax in the British Virgin Islands.**
McWelling Todman, Milton Grundy. Road Town, Tortola: Tortola Trust Corporation, 1978. 30p.
This brief guide by two knowledgeable persons covers the following topics: persons liable for taxation; income; computation; exemptions; rates of tax; and relief for foreign tax.

302 **Report of the Chief Auditor on the accounts of the British Virgin Islands for the year ending 31 December 1987.**
Audit Department, audit certificate by Theodore Fahie, Chief Auditor. Road Town, Tortola: British Virgin Islands Government, 1989. 26p.
The statement of assets and liabilities and the consolidated abstract account are preliminaries. The body of the report is introduced by the text of the statutory duties of the Chief Auditor according to the Audit Ordinance 1971. Other significant sections are: rendition and transmission of accounts; significant account policies; consolidated fund; other public funds – contingencies fund, trust funds, USAID, and Canadian aid; overseas service aid scheme; advances and current accounts; capital fund; investments and cash; deposits; contingent liabilities; all aspects of revenue and expenditure; excess and unauthorized expenditure; summary of recurrent expenditure; supplementary appropriations; summary of capital expenditure; misappropriation of public funds; departmental telephone expenses; statutory authorities and trusts; public accounts committee; and computerization and financial information. The figures are tabulated and in some instances include comparisons as far back as 1976. The report brings all government monies under strict scrutiny, and even calls attention to the overall increase of telephone costs – up 28.42 per cent in 1987 compared to 1986; it gives advice on curbing any current tendencies for abuse.

# Virgin Islands, US

303 **Learning about our Virgin Islands tax system.**
Edited by Kwame Juan Gracia. St. Croix: Cooperative Extension Service, College of the Virgin Islands, 1980. 16p. (Bulletin no. 2).
With the layman in mind, the editor uses simple and uncomplicated terms and expressions. The art work was done by Jymny Dum.

304 **History of the accounting profession in the Virgin Islands.**
[n.p.]: Virgin Islands Society of Certified Accountants, 1977. 50p.
An overview outlining the struggles and achievements of the profession in the United States Virgin Islands.

305 **The story of the Virgin Islands National Bank.**
E.M. Baa. *Daily News*, (10 Jan. 1968), p. 14.
An extensive article in the special Virgin Islands National Bank supplement, giving the history of the bank which was established in 1935. It succeeded the Danish Bank of the West Indies which operated under a franchise granted by the Danish Government.

306 **The United States Virgin Islands and the Eastern Caribbean.**
Darwin Creque. Philadelphia, Pennsylvania: Whitemore, 1968. 266p.
Deals principally with the Eastern Caribbean and puts particular emphasis on the United States Virgin Islands and the Commonwealth of Puerto Rico. It covers historical accounts up to 1967.

307 **The Virgin Islands budget in brief.**
Office of the Budget Director. Charlotte Amalie, St. Thomas: Government of the Virgin Islands, 1980. 20p.
This is a brief citizen's guide to the Budget. The tables and figures are clearly set out and will assist the layman in tracing the taxes he pays to the Government.

# Trade and Industry

## General

308 **The businessman's OECS guide: a directory of commerce, industry and tourism, 1989-1990.**
Organization of Eastern Caribbean States. St. John's, Antigua: KDK Publications, 1989. 258p. maps.
In this work a number of illustrations, tables, diagrams and maps assist in guiding the reader to pertinent information regarding commerce and industry in the Eastern Caribbean states.

309 **Caribbean business directory, 1988-89.**
Edited by Jeremy Taylor. Grand Cayman, Cayman Islands, British West Indies: Caribbean Publishing Co., 1989. 623p. maps.
The region's most comprehensive business data, incorporating Caribbean yellow pages. The general section includes a Caribbean map, a calendar of business events, direct and access codes, telex access codes, travel tips, a profile of the Caribbean as a whole and of Caribbean business. There are also island profiles, each with sections on government, economy, access and transportation, business, leisure, trends, statistics, and telephone numbers. The British Virgin Islands information appears on pages 84-90 and that concerning the United States Virgin Islands on pages 273-87.

310 **United Nations Conference on Trade and Development.**
New York: United Nations, 1984. 60p.
A reliable collection of statistical data relevant to the analysis of world trade and development. Figures for both British and United States Virgin Islands are included.

# Virgin Islands, UK

**311 British Virgin Islands consumer price index.**
Development Planning Unit. Road Town, Tortola: Chief Minister's Office, British Virgin Islands Government, 1991. 1p.
Published monthly with annual cumulations this document consists of seven major sections: Food, beverage and tobacco; Housing; Furniture and household supplies; Clothing and footwear; Transportation; Services; Miscellaneous and some 237 commodity items. For comparative purposes, this January 1991 index also shows figures for January 1990 and December 1990, thereby facilitating comparison on a monthly and annual basis. For example, in the 'housing section' a decrease of 1.0 per cent is shown on a monthly basis, but on an annual basis there is an increase of 2.2 per cent. The document can be used as a measure of the cost of living, as a guide for decision-making in economic sectors and for adjusting wages. At the end of January, the annual rate of inflation stood at 4.3 per cent.

**312 British Virgin Islands marketing seminar: European market.**
John G. Bertram. Road Town, Tortola: British Virgin Islands Tourist Board, 1991. 25p.
These proceedings of a seminar held at Prospect Reef, Virgin Islands, on 8 January outline trading opportunites for the British Virgin Islands in the European market. Basic trading information is given, such as the names and nationalities of airlines, marketing profiles of countries in Europe, and approachable governments and personnel. Hints on advertising are included, making this a useful guide for small developing businesses.

**313 The British Virgin Islands – on the move again.**
Roger Dawes. In: *British Virgin Islands Tourist Handbook*, edited by Vernon W. Pickering. Road Town, Tortola: Laurel, 1988, p. 71-5.
Dawes explains the reasons behind the British Virgin Islands' optimism in the international business world.

**314 Construction seminar planned.**
*British Virgin Island Beacon*, vol. 7 no. 12 (30 Aug. 1990), p. 13.
Outlined here is the goal of a seminar sponsored by the British Virgin Islands Hotel and Commerce Association on Virgin Gorda on 1 September 1990: 'to develop a "safe framework within which the construction industry can work and grow"'. The concerns dealt with include: increasing labour requirements; regulation of building plans, and the demands of architects, draughtsmen and project managers.

**315 Economic and business report of the Virgin Islands.**
Tony Thorndike. In: *The Latin American and Caribbean Review*. NTC Business Books (a division of NTC Publishing Group), 1989, p. 140-1, 190-1.
In each instance, with the British Virgin Islands appearing first, followed by the United States Virgin Islands, the author outlines the current political, social and financial concerns; gives the country file with key facts, for example, the size, population, chief town and year of discovery; and a guide to businesses on the islands.

316 **New insurance legislation.**
Government of the British Virgin Islands.   In: *News Release*, no. 79R/
91 (29 April 1991) p. 1-2.
The Insurance Business (Special Provisions) Act 1991 'will enable the Insurance
Supervisor to investigate in detail all the Insurance Companies registered in the British
Virgin Islands'. The release also states that the legislation applies equally to onshore
and offshore insurance business and all local brokers and agents, together with the
companies they represent, will have to apply for approval; that it is a preliminary Act
to provide powers to investigate and, if necessary, close down any of the 1500
insurance companies registered in the islands; that it should give the public greater
confidence than they have had in the past, when buying their insurance policies; and
that a more detailed Insurance Act which is expected to create an attractive environment
for legitimate insurance business, is being prepared for release later in the year.

317 **Offer of products.**
British Virgin Islands Commerce Assocation.   *Bulletin Board* (First
quarter, 1991), p. 1-5.
One of the initial efforts of the Association, this list of international manufacturers and
service personnel with addresses, descriptions of products and of expertise, will serve
the young business community well.

318 **OECS/Caribbean Expo '91**
Government Information Office.   *News Release*, no. 100R/91 (23 May
1991), p. 1-2.
An exciting event is announced – the second OECS/Caribbean Expo, which is to be
held in Antigua from 30 May to 3 June and which will be a showcase for all types of
regional goods, investment opportunities and services available for export trade within
and outside the region. Ten companies from the British Virgin Islands are
participating. During the five-day period, the trade and investment seminars which are
planned include topics such as: exportation; entrepreneurship development; telecommunications in the Caribbean; credit guarantee schemes; investing in the Eastern
Caribbean opportunity zone, the common external tariff and implications for OECS
manufacturers. The exhibition is being sponsored by OECS states including the British
Virgin Islands.

319 **Planters' and merchants' everyday life and business in the British
Virgin Islands 200 years ago.**
Vernon Pickering.   In: *British Virgin Islands Tourist Handbook*. Edited
by Vernon W. Pickering. Road Town, Tortola: Laurel, 1988. p. 93-108.
In this article, Pickering explores the imports and exports of a tiny British colony
during the plantation era. It describes inter-island trade and the routes of the Tortola
commercial fleet of two centuries ago.

320 **The regulation of insurance and banking business in the British Virgin
Islands.**
St. John's, Antigua: Eastern Caribbean Common Market, 1980. 8p.
Banking systems, insurance, economic resources, interest rates and economic
development are all defined in this document.

# Boating

321  **Final report on the advice to the government of the British Virgin
Islands on the Pleasure Boat (Yachting) Industry.**
Ivor L. Jackson.   Road Town, Tortola: Commonwealth Fund for
Technical Cooperation, 1982.

With numerous tables to assist, this report covers in great detail the management
techniques and various development projects which the pleasure-boat industry would
involve.

322  **Sailing: one of the main attractions.**
Rachael Jackson.   *Financial Times* (29 June 1990), p. 3.

Jackson attributes the magnificently unspoilt state of the islands to the development of
the bareboat industry. Other contributors to the economy are also examined.

323  **Study of mini-cruise ships: British Virgin Islands.**
Ivor Jackson.   St. Johns, Antigua: Ivor Jackson and Associates, 1987.
35p. maps.

The terms of reference called for were: The context in which recommendations made
in the Jackson 1981 report and 1982 advisory mission on the yachting industry were
implemented; Conflicts between the yachting and scuba-diving industries and the
growth of mini-cruise ships; Economic and environmental impacts of the mini-cruise
ships in the territory; and Infrastructural needs of the subsector. The study was carried
out within the context of the wider-based tourism industry, paying suitable attention to
relationships with other sectors.

324  **World's largest charter company grows.**
*BVI Beacon*, vol. 5, no. 20 (27 Oct. 1988), p. 1.

The history and development of Moorings Ltd, described as the largest charter
company in the world. The company was founded by members of the Carey family in
1969.

# Cottage industries

325  **Art craft industry.**
Peter Wallum, assisted by J. Gordon-Russel.   Road Town, Tortola:
British Virgin Islands Government, 1978. 48p. maps.

Wallum outlines existing modes and practice in the art/craft sector and offers
suggestions for improving output, display and marketing.

326 **Development proposal for mineral water purification, ice making and ferry service in the British Virgin Islands.**
Peter Wallum. Road Town, Tortola: British Virgin Islands Government, 1978. 8p.
A very feasible proposal which puts profitable businesses within the reach of the small-scale entrepreneur. Although the proposal is now more than a decade old, there are some suggestions which local operators could still apply to improve services for the benefit and safety of all – especially with regard to ferry services.

327 **British Virgin Islands batik: a new local industry.**
Claudia Colli. *Virgin Islander* (Aug. 1980), p. 11.
The writer describes a government project that made a beautiful impact on the lives of young women in several rural villages.

328 **The bottle industry.**
Ermin Burnett. *Virgin Islands Historical Documents*, vol. 3, no. 1 (May 1990), p. 3-7.
A splendid article describing the development of a cottage industry in which both groups of Virgin Islands participated from the 1950s onwards. The United States Virgin Islanders produced a cologne for men from the bay rum plant, and British Virgin Islands women wove straw over the bottles to contain the cologne. The production steps are outlined and are also highlighted by illustrations which generally enhance the article.

329 **The Callwood distillery.**
Claudia Colli. *British Virgin Island Welcome Magazine*, vol. 14, no. 2 (Feb.-March 1985), p. 11.
A lively survey describing two hundred years of rum making in the islands. It locates the rum distilleries, their techniques and apparatuses as well as including personages and anecdotes from across the territory.

330 **The living legend of Salt Island.**
Claudia Colli. *British Virgin Islander*, no. 6 (1974), p. 6.
A true picture of the pomp and glory of the ceremony and activities surrounding 'reaping the salt' on Salt Island. It describes an ancient industry which occupies a mere handful of people resident on the island but which also ensures that Her Majesty the Queen gets her traditional due at each reaping.

331 **Souvenir industries for the British Virgin Islands.**
Braham D. Kapur, S. Sen Gupta. Road Town, Tortola: CFTC, 1978. 12p.
Enterprising and imaginative, this joint report is a compilation of ideas for small-scale industries which entrepreneurs could launch comfortably, without too much of a financial struggle.

# Virgin Islands, US

**332  Amerada Hess Corporation settled its contract dispute with the U.S. Virgin Islands Government.**
*Caribbean Monthly Bulletin*, vol. 15, no. 6 (June 1981), p. 14-17.
This item reports that Amerada Hess Corporation, which operates the world's largest oil refinery on the island of St. Croix, United States Virgin Islands, settled its contract with the United States Virgin Islands Government in May 1981. The new contract stipulates that Hess will pay a two cents per barrel fee on oil produced; pay more than double its current level of property taxes (to total around US$10 million); increase employment training and hiring for technical supervisory and management positions; construct a vocational school; sell fuel below market price to the Water and Power Authorities; and resume the expansion of the factory. The report also carries two articles on the contract dispute, originally published in the *Multinational Monitor* magazine. Their titles are: 'Hess twin tactics: play island against island, bypass United States shipping costs' by Steve Koester; and 'Amerada Hess: showdown in the Virgin Islands' by Matthew Rothschild.

**333  The bay oil industry of St. John, United States Virgin Islands.**
Earl Shaw.  *Economic Geography*, vol. 10 (1934), p. 143-6.
An account of a then thriving industry produced from the indigenous bay plant of St. John.

**334  The Caribbean Basin Initiative.**
Alexander Farrelly.  *Vital Speeches* (15 Nov. 1987), p. 68-73.
This verbatim item is the territory's current Governor's assessment of expected benefits to be derived from the Virgin Islands involvement with the Caribbean Basin Initiative (CBI).

**335  Retailing in paradise.**
David P. Schulz.  *Stores*, vol. 70 (April 1988), p. 63-73.
Looks at retailing in the United States Virgin Islands with relevant references to the Clothing Studio, A.H. Riise's Company of St. Thomas, and to problems of hiring staff.

**336  Traditional cottage industries of the Virgin Islands.**
Jeannette Allis.  Charlotte Amalie, St. Thomas: Division of Libraries, Museums and Archaeological Services, 1986. 30p. bibliog.
An ingenious cultural calendar with descriptions of how to do island industries for each month of the year. For example, fishnet making; joinery; needlecrafts; boat building; basketry; charcoal making; bay rum making; broom making, etc. It is well illustrated and 'cultural quotes' are also included in the daily entries of the calendar.

**337  United States Virgin Islands.**
Kenneth A. Rosskopf.  *Business America*, vol. 17 (17 Sept. 1984), p. 3-8.
Rosskopf explains why the United States Virgin Islands is a leading location for foreign sales corporations.

338 **United States Virgin Islands launches new industrial development programme.**
Eric Dawson.    *Barrons*, vol. 67 (2 Nov. 1987), p. 63-5.

Dawson gives a brief outline of this proposed development project in St.Thomas; he states the objectives and the benefits. Other business sites are also illustrated in a special advertising section.

339 **Virgin Islands corporation laws.**
United States Virgin Islands Government.    New York: Butterworth Legal Publications, 1985. 200p.

This publication brings together all the laws that govern the establishing and the operating of companies and corporations in the United States Virgin Islands.

# Agriculture and Fisheries

## General

**340 Agricultural problems of small states with special reference to Commonwealth Caribbean countries.**
B. Persaud. London: Commonwealth Secretariat, 1987. 16p.
Persaud outlines agricultural problems in small states and touches on some solutions in order to maximize the agricultural potential of the territories. The paper was presented at a symposium of economic development and prospects of the OECS states.

**341 Pasture research and development in the Eastern Caribbean.**
St. Johns, Antigua: Caribbean Research and Development Institute (CARDI), 1986. 47p.
Concentrates on grazing patterns in the Eastern Caribbean as input to the Forage Seed Production Project, funded by the European Development Fund (EDF). The findings should benefit the grass improvement programme of the British Virgin Islands Agricultural Department.

**342 Cropping systems in the tropics.**
Shirley Evelyn. St. Augustine, Trinidad: University of the West Indies, 1989. 64p.
Evelyn, a University librarian, is an expert in Caribbean bibliography and has compiled several subject bibliographies over the years. This one is a list of references to cropping systems carried out in the tropics and cited in the Caribbean Agricultural Information System database for the years 1980-88. Reference to it would familiarize agriculturalists with developments in the field, and could avoid unnecessary duplication of effort, research and experiment in individual agricultural departments throughout the region.

# Virgin Islands, UK

343 **Agricultural Exhibition, Industry and Nutrition Week: develop British Virgin Islands wealth through agriculture, industry and health.**
Road Town, Tortola: British Virgin Islands Department of Agriculture, 1987. 24p.

Intended to capture the spirit of the week's theme, to convey useful agricultural and nutritional information, and to serve as a handbook for planning future exhibitions. In addition to the usual food and livestock produce, the exhibition itself featured a variety of local skills, handicrafts and art. Seminar–workshops conducted by the Eastern Caribbean Centre for Learning under the auspices of the University of the Virgin Islands were also featured. Professional staff gave lectures and demonstrations in soil testing, tree grafting, apiculture, cultivation of the sweet potato, livestock science, youth activities, and other topics. All this is captured in this illustrated and very well-produced memento.

344 **Agriculture in the British Virgin Islands.**
E. Noel Vanterpool.   Road Town, Tortola: Agricultural Department, 1977. 11p.

Noel Vanterpool, then Chief Agriculture Officer of the territory, presents a picture to the Economic Advisory Committee, describing the role of agriculture in the overall development of the territory. He speaks of the present structure of agriculture, future capabilities, problems encountered, and possible solutions.

345 **Agricultural resources may be under-utilized.**
National Parks Trust.   *Resource*, vol. 2, no. 2 (April-June 1984), p. 1, 4.

The article analyses expenditures on food imports against the current underuse of land and sea resources, taking for example the small acreage of various units of fruit-growing trees. It makes recommendations for increased agricultural productivity to meet escalating local demands.

346 **Agricultural survey of the British Virgin Islands for 1981.**
Road Town, Tortola: British Virgin Islands Department of Agriculture, 1981. 64p. maps.

This report records the results of a survey conducted between 29 March and 30 July 1981. The data were collected by professional agricultural officers who visited and interviewed every farmer on the island. The project represents timely and accurate data on agricultural production, costs and returns, number of farmers, farmers' activities, consumption, demand, exports, imports, problems that farmers encounter, and other statistics. The report is a form of farmers' registration and identification, but it is also a useful reference tool for farmers claiming compensation in times of crop damage and for livestock immunization programmes.

347 **Edible fruits and vegetables of the English-speaking Caribbean.**
Devi P.V. Prasad.   Kingston, Jamaica: Caribbean Food and Nutrition
Institute, PAHO/WHO, 1986. 68p.

This text, which is well illustrated with pictures, tables and diagrams, describes
Caribbean fruits and vegetables and gives their nutritional value. It is a useful guide for
students, dietitians, agriculturalists and farmers.

348 **Hydroponic gardening.**
Minine Norgrove.   *Resource*, vol. 2, no. 1 (1984), p. 5.

The author, a successful gardener and landscaper, explains the ABC of hydroponic
gardening, some of which she learnt at the gardening exhibition at EPCOT, Disney
World, Florida.

349 **Livestock development.**
M.F. Watson.   Road Town, Tortola: British Development in the
Caribbean, 1974. 3p.

Briefly describes prevalent trends, encourages the revitalization of traditional methods
and also suggests alternative methods of improving livestock in the British Virgin
Islands.

350 **Report of the Department of Agriculture.**
Road Town, Tortola: Department of Agriculture, 1980. 16p.

Reviews the work of the Department for the year 1980 and includes crop production;
government nurseries; agricultural extension; crop pathology; fisheries; co-operative
development; agriculture and livestock capital projects; and abattoir and agricultural
exhibitions.

**British Virgin Islands: territorial report for the year 1987.**
*See* item no. 9.

**Tourism management and environmental and developmental issues.**
*See* item no. 79.

**Common trees of Puerto Rico and the Virgin Islands.**
*See* item no. 83.

Flora and fauna section.
*See* items 85-9, 92-6.

**Cagrindex: abstracts of the agricultural literature of the Caribbean.**
*See* item no. 603.

# Virgin Islands, US

351  **Agriculture and food fair of the Virgin Islands.**
St. Croix: Department of Agriculture, Virgin Islands of the United
States, 1977. [n.p.].
This is an illustrated annual which celebrates the island's agricultural produce. The title
varies; for example, 'Agriculture and foodfair of St. Croix, Virgin Islands', in 1971-73;
'St. Croix Agriculture and foodfair' in 1974; and 'Virgin Islands Agricultural foodfair'
in 1975-76.

352  **Avocado production and marketing.**
Chris Ramcharan, Clinton George, George Morris, foreword by D.S.
Padda, edited by Liz Wilson.  Kingshill, St Croix: Cooperative
Extension Service, College of the Virgin Islands, 1983. 18p. bibliog.
(Extension Bulletin, no. 4.)
All essential information for the successful production of the avocado is presented in
clearly set out and easy-to-follow paragraphs under general sections: avocado
production; economics of avocado production; recipes. The work is well produced and
is illustrated with many tables and figures, making it an inspirational booklet for
anyone interested in growing fruit and vegetables.

353  **Essentials of farm financial management.**
George Morris, Randall Macedon.  *Farm Management Factsheet*,
no. 1 (Feb. 1984), p. 1-5.
Specialists in the field, Morris and Macedon explain financial procedure as it relates to
the farming business. They give details of accounting methods; essential farm records;
income statements; revenue; adjustment; balance sheets; assets and liabilities, and
conclude with an actual income statement and balance sheet.

354  **Gardeners' Factsheet.**
St.Croix: Cooperative Extension Service, 1979- . irregular.
Each factsheet surveys one aspect of gardening and contains extremely detailed and
useful information on that aspect's method and application. Well designed and
illustrated, they are produced by specialists in agriculture, and can include up to four
pages, which could be secured in ring-binders. Some examples of topics and authors
already published: Vegetable planting and harvest guide. Gardeners' Factsheet, no. 1
(Jan. 1979); Growing vegetable slips. no. 3 (Jan. 1979); Transplanting vegetable crops.
no. 4 (Feb. 1979); Mulch for your garden. no. 5 (Feb. 1979); How to prepare your
own compost. no. 6 (Feb. 1976); Staking and training tomato plants. no. 7 (March
1979); Growing spinach in the Virgin Islands. no. 10 (May 1979); Controlling
nematodes in the vegetable garden. no. 11 (June 1979); and Organic gardening: soil
fertility. no. 18 (Sept. 1979). All of these are by John M. Guber. Christopher
Ramcharan has produced: Propagation of fruit and ornamental plants by cutting.
no. 12 (June 1979); Propagation of fruit and ornamental plants by layering. no. 13
(July 1979); Propagation of fruit and ornamental plants by grafting. no. 14 (Aug.
1979); Propagation of fruit and ornamental plants by budding. no. 15 (Sept. 1979); and
Fertilizing your garden for optimum yields. no. 16 (Sept. 1979). Others in the series
are: Organic gardening: pest control. no. 19 (Oct. 1979); and A simple homedrip

irrigation system. no. 20. (Oct. 1979) by Michael A. Ivie, illustrated by Gene Zegetosky; Growing mangoes. no. 21 (March 1990) by Christopher Ramcharan; Growing citrus. no. 22 (April 1990) by Eric Dillingham; Growing mesples (Sapodillas) no. 24 (Jan. 1982) by Clinton George; Testing soils for better yields; part 1. no. 25 (Feb. 1983); Interpreting your soil testing results. part 2. no. 26 (Feb. 1983) by Kim Stearman. The series is a major leap forward in assisting and promoting self-sufficiency.

355 **Sorrel production and marketing in the United States Virgin Islands.**
Clinton George, George Morris, foreword by Darshan S. Padda, edited by Liz Wilson. Kingshill, St. Croix: Cooperative Extension Service, College of the Virgin Islands, 1984. 14p. (Extension Bulletin, no. 5).
Sorrel production is explained under several headings: description, cultivars, soils and climate, land preparation and planting, fertilizing, pests and diseases, harvesting and yield. The economics of production are calculated in gross receipts, viable cost, returns, other factors affecting cost and return, marketing and processing potential. There are also useful recipes and an abundance of tables, figures and other illustrations. The attractive sorrel plant with its red fruits, white flowers and green elongated leaves, makes an eye-catching design for the cover.

**Farm Management Factsheet.**
*See* item no. 577.

**Fish and Wildlife News.**
*See* item no. 578.

**Agricultural research directory.**
*See* item no. 596.

# Land development schemes

356 **Development and land use programme for the British Virgin Islands.**
Henry Klumb, Melton Cobin, Robert Fisher, in consultation with Herbert Croucher. [n.p.]: Klumb and Stantaton Robins, 1960. 54p.
Presents the general background and status of the British Virgin Islands and outlines land-use recommendations which would 'assist the people to inprove their economy and raise their standard of living by more intensive use of their limited resources'. The report was accepted in principle by the government and it would be interesting to discover how many of the recommendations were put into practice.

357 **Report of the Anegada Land Commission.**
Barry Renwick.    Road Town, Tortola: British Virgin Islands
Government, 1987. 20p.

Prepared by the former justice Barry Renwick, the report lists five findings and
recommendations: the title to land is governed by the Land Adjudication Ordinance
1970 and the Registered Land Ordinance 1970; a land-use plan should be created with
the support of the majority of Anegadians; the walls (land contained by walls) should
be vested in their owners if positive ownership can be proved; the government should
appoint an Advisory Development Committee; and incentives should be given to
Anegadian developers. The report also gives the legal history of Anegada land
onwership, from the Real Property Limitation Act 1833 to the Penn versus Stevens
Privy Council Appeal 27 (1985).

358 **Land grant programmes in action.**
Edited by Liz Wilson, foreword by Arthur A. Richards.    St. Croix:
College of the Virgin Islands Cooperative Extension Service, 1982. 36p.

The programmes and services of a land-grant institution are explained in articles and
photographs. The role of the land-grant programmes is defined by Darshan Padda (the
Director) as research, extension and teaching. The basic studies and education
programmes are built upon the consideration that land, water, energy and capital are
limited; local food production must increase to diversify and stabilize the economy;
basic natural resources must be conserved; human nutrition research and education
must focus on local consumption patterns; effective youth development is critical to the
continued development of future leadership capabilities. Programmes and outlines are
given and include horticulture, pest and pesticide management, agronomy, animal
science, aquaculture, home economics, community resource development. The
programmes are useful not only to students enrolled on academic courses but also on a
more informal basis to the residents of the community.

# Forestry

359 **Forestry in the Leeward Islands: the British Virgin Islands.**
J.S. Beard.    Port-of-Spain, Trinidad: [n.p.], 1945. 16p.

Accounts for the sparsity of woodland and locates and describes the remains of a
primeval forest on Sage Mountain, Tortola, British Virgin Islands. This report, by the
conservator of forests for the region, was made after a preliminary visit to the islands.
It is a Supplement to Bulletin No. 7A: Development and Welfare in the West Indies.

# Food, nutrition, recipes

360 **Directory of food, nutrition and dietetics training programmes in institutions/departments of nutrition, dietetics and home economics in the Caribbean region.**
Eunice Warner, Manuelita Zephirin.   Kingston, Jamaica: Caribbean Food and Nutrition Institute, 1987. 159p.
A useful guide which describes the content and duration of courses dealing with food, nutrition and training available in well-established institutions throughout the Caribbean.

361 **Caribbean Diet Digest.**
Frederiksted, St. Croix: Caribbean Diet Institute, 1981- . quarterly.
Edited by Dorene E. Carter, this publication focuses on a crucial area: the food and nutritional concerns of the people of the Virgin Islands and the Caribbean, and seeks to 'improve the health of residents'. Topics relating to the United States Virgin Islands get special treatment, and articles on nutrition, feeding the elderly, recipes of notable cooks, reviews of culinary books, and announcements of health programmes, make this a useful and interesting item. Available from: Caribbean Diet Digest, PO Box 191, Frederiksted, St. Croix, United States Virgin Islands, 00840.

362 **Famous native recipes of the Virgin Islands.**
Dea Murray.   St. Thomas: Paper Book Gallery, 1968. 32p.
This is an exciting collection of recipes gathered from outstanding cooks on St. Thomas, St. Croix and St. John. It is illustrated.

363 **Famous rum drinks of the Virgin Islands.**
Dea Murray.   [n.p.], Florida: Dukane, 1970. 32p.
These recipes were collected from popular hotels, restaurants and bars in the Virgin Islands.

364 **Native recipes.**
Cooperation Extension Services, foreword by Darshan S. Padda, introduction by Olivia Henry.   St. Croix: College of the Virgin Islands, 1985. rev. ed. 98p.
This revised booklet of native recipes – put out by the Home Economics component of the extension service of the College of the Virgin Islands – is an attempt to assist Virgin Islanders to improve their diets through the use of local products and cooking methods developed over the years. It is illustrated and includes a glossary and index.

365 **The Virgin Islands cook-house cook-book.**
Doris Jadan, Ivan Jadan.   Cruz Bay, St. John: The authors, 1973. 91p.
A spiral-bound illustrated collection of native recipes, many of which were first tried by the authors.

366 **Virgin Islands native recipes.**
Women's League of Voters. Charlotte Amalie, St. Thomas: Carib
Graphic Arts, 1956. rev. ed. 48p.

First published in 1954, this authentic collection was later revised and enlarged by a
very influential group in Virgin Islands society.

# Fisheries

## General

367 **An assessment of the mariculture potential of the indigenous Eastern
Caribbean brine shrimp.**
Melvin H. Goodwin, Euna Moore, Thomas Nun. Red Hook, St.
Thomas: Island Resources Foundation, 1984. 117p.

All member countries of the Organization of Eastern Caribbean States, including the
British Virgin Islands, are covered in this assessment. The topics discussed are: general
marine resources, shellfish culture and shrimps.

368 **Leeward Island fisheries.**
Nigel Peacock. Road Town, Tortola: Ministry of Overseas
Development for British Virgin Islands Government, 1976. 19p.

Lays down basic rules and procedures for the management and development of
fisheries in the islands.

## Virgin Islands, UK

369 **Geographical distribution of the ciguatoxin fish in the eastern half of the
British Virgin Islands.**
William Davin. Master's thesis, University of Mississippi, 1977. 42p.

The thesis is based on the examination of thirty stations in the eastern half of the
British Virgin Islands for ciguatoxin fish collected with fish traps. The stations along
the 100-fathom contour were found to be the most toxic ones.

370 **Status of British Virgin Islands fisheries development.**
Randolph Walters.   In: *Report of proceedings on: OECS workshop for the formulation of a regional management and development programme for fisheries of the OECS region held July 30 – August 1.*   Castries, St. Lucia: OECS Secretariat, 1986, p. 1-3 of Appendix D.

This status report describes the components of the fishing industry in the British Virgin Islands. The author covers fishing vessels, fishery development and marketing potential.

# Transport and Communications

## Virgin Islands, UK

371  **Beef Island airport: British Virgin Islands.**
Canadian International Development Agency.    Ottawa: Airports
Authority Group, 1987. 68p. maps.
The diversity of the functional areas of an airport is reflected in this report which
proposes ways to minimize land-use conflicts, provides adequate protected areas for
the requirements of key aviation facilities, and provides adequate supplies of
marketable land for commercial development. It will continue to serve as a useful
framework within which future project proposals may be evaluated, providing that the
plan is updated to keep abreast with changing requirements.

372  **Port engineering study.**
Wolfe Barry and Partners.    London; Road Town, Tortola: Ministry of
Communications, Works and Public Utilities, 1985. 200p.
Explores the feasibility of extending port and marine facilities for the British Virgin
Islands. It also describes some port-related vessels and includes cost estimates for the
project.

373  **Review of maritime sector of the British Virgin Islands for the**
**establishment of a marine department.**
B.M. Sallah.    London: CFTC for British Virgin Islands Government,
1984. 65p.
In his review Sallah looks at the historical role of maritime facilities in the islands and
emphasizes the importance of development to facilitate their expanding role in tourism
and trade. He touches on the need to introduce enabling maritime legislation.

374  **Schedules one, two and three to the vehicles and road traffic regulations.**
Traffic Section of the Police Department.   Road Town, Tortola:
British Virgin Islands Government, 1973. 28p.
A guide to the traffic signs and their meanings. The illustrations are in colour.

375  **ZBVI: twenty five years and still going strong.**
Jasmine David.   *Island Sun* (5 May 1990), p. 1, 2.
A brief history of the only radio station in the British Virgin Islands, on its twenty-fifth anniversary.

**Caribbean handbook, 1986.**
*See* item no. 2.

**The Commonwealth year book, 1990.**
*See* item no. 4.

**British Virgin Islands: territorial report for the year 1987.**
*See* item no. 9.

**Discover.**
*See* item no. 10.

# Virgin Islands, US

376  **Airlines fight to dominate the United States Virgin Islands market.**
Adele Schwartz.   *Air Transport World*, vol. 21 (June 1984), p. 84-6.
Schwartz shows how three airlines – Virgin Seaplane Shuttle, Virgin Air and Sunaire – vie for command of inter-island traffic feeding the hubs of St. Thomas and St. Croix.

377  **Caribbean basin becomes large telecommunications market.**
Ted Johnston.   *Telematics and Information*, vol. 7, no. 1 (1990),
p. 1-7.
Johnson shows how the Caribbean Basin Initiative (CBI) has extended to the region many benefits beyond trade expansion. Among the new investments associated with the CBI, are a number of projects to expand and improve both regional telecommunications and telecommunication projects within individual countries. Projects to improve the British and United States Virgin Islands systems are listed on page 3, under the heading: 'Major telecommunications projects underway'.

# Labour, Employment and Manpower

## Virgin Islands, UK

378 **Employment in the British Virgin Islands.**
Labour Commissioner's Office.    Road Town, Tortola: British Virgin
Islands Government, 1973. 62p.

Conducted in June 1973, this employment survey studies and compares the labour
force at the census of 1970 with that in 1973. It includes statistics on the issue of work
permits by the Labour Department and on unemployment in the territory.

379 **Human resources development planning.**
Salasan Associates Inc.    Road Town: Tortola, British Virgin Islands
Government, 1987.

The Human Resources Development policy was developed during a national
consultation on the topic held earlier in the year. It outlines the basic principles on
which a modern developmental human resource management system will be built. The
document recognizes the need to develop, as soon as is feasible, detailed operational
policies, procedures and mechanisms which will assist managers in achieving more
effective planning in the British Virgin Islands.

380 **Labour Code Ordinance, 1975.**
Legislature of the Virgin Islands.    Road Town, Tortola: British Virgin
Islands Government, 1975. 84p.

The Ordinance brings together – in terms appropriate for the present state of the
economy of the British Virgin Islands – all legislation applicable to employment
standards and industrial relations. The Code has six divisions. 'National policy' sets
out the expressions of national policy to be used in the various provisions of the Code;
'Administration' sets out the principles governing the administration of the Code;

'Basic employment' deals with discrimination, working conditions, contracts, termination, leave privileges, national minimum wage, penalties, unfair dismissals; 'Employment, health, safety and welfare'; 'Women, young persons and children (Employment)'; and 'Work permits' which deals with applications, penalties and forms.

381   **Labour Department: report for the year 1987.**
Labour Department.   Road Town, Tortola: British Virgin Islands Government, 1988. 14p.
The functions of the Labour Department are described, including: to receive, record and investigate complaints with respect to employer–employee relations and make efforts to dispose of the issues raised by voluntary adjustment of settlement; to process work permit applications and collect work permit fees. There are two main sections: administration and a general review. The latter reviews employment; industrial relations; labour relations service; industrial action; labour inspection service; inspection visits; international labour standards; employment service and work permits. Analyses of work permits issued are given in the following tables: Work permits granted by nationality and race; Classification of work permits by type and sex; Classification of work permits by types of permits and by status; . . . by occupational classification; . . . sex and country of origin; . . . by month, status and type. Useful appendixes include: Analysis of infringements observed in 1987; persons registered seeking work in 1985, 1986 and 1987 by month and sex; persons placed in jobs in 1985, 1986 and 1987; work permit fees collected by month and island; list of conventions applicable to the BVIs.

**British Virgin Islands: territorial report for the year 1987.**
*See* item no. 9.

**1980-1991 population census of the Commonwealth Caribbean: British Virgin Islands, volume one.**
*See* item no. 157.

**Speech from the throne.**
*See* item no. 273.

**Budget address 1991.**
*See* item no. 299.

**Communication.**
*See* item no. 469.

# Virgin Islands, US

382   **The British West Indian alien labour problem in the Virgin Islands.**
James W. Green.   *Caribbean Studies*, vol. 12, no. 4 (Jan. 1973), p. 56-75.
Emigrant workers in a foreign country are transient; some of the problems engendered are sympathetically discussed.

**Labour, Employment and Manpower.** Virgin Islands, US

383 **A household survey of the Virgin Islands on economic development.**
Frank Mills and the Office of Policy Planning and Research of the
Department of Commerce. Charlotte Amalie, St. Thomas: Economic
Policy Council, 1978. 128p.
Numerous tables help to elucidate the factual details of this survey; the emphasis is on
employment situations.

**America's Virgin Islands: a history of human rights and wrongs.**
*See* item no. 145.

**A profile of Frederiksted, St. Croix, United States Virgin Islands.**
*See* item no. 291.

**Virgin Islands Employment Security Agency Bulletin.**
*See* item no. 591.

**Virgin Islands Labour Market Review.**
*See* item no. 592.

# Environment

384 **Island environments and development.**
Christopher Howell, E. Towle.   St. Thomas: Islands Resources
Foundation, 1976. maps. 18, 124p.

This far-reaching work studies the exploitation of mineral resources; management of man-made resources and disposal of waste; management of natural renewable resources (including water, soil, flora and fauna); conservation of areas of outstanding aesthetic or scientific value; the preservation of historical sites and other cultural property. There are recommendations at the end of each section.

385 **Natural resources of the British Virgin Islands.**
Nicolas Clarke, Bertrand Lettsome.   Road Town, Tortola: Laurel,
1989. 44p. bibliog.

Prepared for the Environmental Science Programme which was organized with the Department of Education and Culture, this is a collection of essays on various aspects of the environment in the British Virgin Islands. The authors are experts in conservation matters and have written extensively in periodical literature.

386 **Cane Garden Bay.**
Mary White, foreword by Ivor Jackson.   Road Town, Tortola: British
Virgin Islands Parks Trust under Eastern Caribbean Natural Areas
Management Programmme for the British Virgin Islands Parks and
Protected Areas Project, 1983. 32p.

Based on the results of an exhibition on the history, culture and life of the Cane Garden Bay community in 1983, the work describes the factors that contribute to the cohesiveness of that community. It deals with natural history, cultural history, the economy and activities. There is also a directory of useful information on the community. It is delicately illustrated, with graphics produced by Natalie Clarke.

387 **North Sound, Virgin Gorda: British Virgin Islands.**
Nicolas Clarke, Tighe Geoghegan, illustrated by Katherine Turner,
calligraphy by Jean Leslie, photographs by Nick Clarke, cover design
by John Turner. British Virgin Islands National Parks Trust and
Eastern Caribbean Natural Area Management Programme, 12456/-.
1986. 36p. map.
This short guide explores North Sound, Virgin Gorda, from the point of view of a
naturalist, looking at land, sky and beneath the sea. One of the safest anchorages in
the Caribbean Sea, North Sound has been designated by the Government as a
hurricane shelter.

388 **Virgin anchorages.**
C.G. Cary. Road Town, Tortola: The Moorings Ltd, 1974. 80p.
A photographic guide in full colour to the most popular anchorages in the Virgin
Islands.

# Town and country planning

## Virgin Islands, UK

389 **East End/Long Look master plan.**
Town and Country Planning Department. Road Town, Tortola:
British Virgin Islands Government, 1979. 35p. maps.
A plan showing the minutest details of the development of the second largest
residential area in the territory. It allows for the environmental conservation of the
district with its numerous bays, harbours, reefs and mangroves. Suggestions are made
for the inclusion of cultural crafts, foods and services in various amenities and shops. It
is useful for comparison with current development trends in the area.

390 **Wickhams Cay: a seventy acre town centre development.**
Frank Knight and Rutley. London: Frank Knight and Rutley for the
British Virgin Islands Government, 1975. 13p.
A report on the management of the Wickhams Cay development project during the
years 1973 and 1974. It would be useful to compare the findings of this report with the
actual development as it finally evolved.

## Virgin Islands, US

391 **Three towns: conservation and renewal of Charlotte Amalie,**
**Christiansted, and Frederiksted of the United States Virgin Islands.**
Edited by Ole Svensson. Copenhagen: Department of Town
Planning, Royal Danish Academy of Fine Arts, 1965. 122p. maps.
A team of architects, architectural historians and town planners was formed to find
solutions to the common problems associated with the vigorous building activities of
the 1960s and 1970s which seemed to overwhelm the historical quaintness of the
architecture in all three towns. The authors present an engaging study of each town,
detailing the history, structure, road system, character and planning problems of each
urban cluster. Maps showing the use of structures, their structural quality and their
height accompany the text, and it is also illustrated with diagrams showing ground
values, an industrial survey and land-use proposals. Precise recommmendations are
given for each town and the last two chapters, which deal with conservation and
renewal, also recommend that protective regulations be imposed on privately owned
buildings worthy of conservation. Generally, the work presents proposals which
enhance the architectural legacy of the towns as well as their economic potential. The
book should still be of great interest to Caribbeanists and town planners.

# Housing and architecture

## Virgin Islands, UK

392 **Caribbean style.**
Suzanne Slesin, Stafford Cliff, Jack Berthelot, Martine Gaume, Daniel
Chabaneix, illustrated by Gilles de Chabaneix, foreword by Jan
Morris. New York: Clarkson N. Potter, 1985. 290p. maps.
Offers information on island vegetation and colours, plantation houses, town houses,
popular houses, contemporary houses and gardens. Foreign and island influences are
also reflected. In addition, the section called 'Architectural notebook' provides plans
and information on different types of houses on various islands. The architecture of the
entire Caribbean is portrayed in over 600 exquisite full-colour photographs of houses,
flowers, sky and sea.

393 **Housing programmes and policies in the British Virgin Islands: a**
**perspective for twenty-eight years (1973-2000).**
C.M. Palvia. Bridgetown, Barbados: UNDP, 1973. 35p.
This document outlines the current housing situation, assesses needs, develops housing
policy and advises on long-term housing programmes including low-income housing if
this becomes necessary.

394 **Landscapes of the past.**
Sheila Hyndman. *Welcome Magazine*, vol. 20, no. 2 (Feb.-March 1991), p. 5-11.
Beautifully written and charmingly illustrated, this article preserves the varied construction techniques and architectural styles which evolved down the centuries. From thatch and wattle to wooden frames and hip roofs (galvanized or shingled), from concrete and columned arcades to bricks and lattice, methods and styles are skilfully described using some of the classic tradtional houses as examples. Researched and written by one of the islands' most talented writers, this article shows that the traditional West Indian architecture is still dominating the landscape, a trend that augurs well for 'asserting a proud past and preserving a rich culture'.

# Virgin Islands, US

395 **Historic buildings of St. Thomas and St. John.**
Frederik C. Gjessing, William P. MacClean. London; Basingstoke: Macmillan Caribbean, 1967. 106p.
Illustrates and gives the historical background of: the commercial district; military structures; public buildings; churches and chapels; urban residences; plantations; styles and contrasts. There is also a glossary and a list of additional reading on the subject.

396 **The three quarters of the town of Charlotte Amalie.**
Edith de Jough Woods. Rome: MAPes MONDe, 1989. 158p. maps.
This work tells the history of the colonial seaport town on the island of St. Thomas. It also studies the architectural details and forms that have endured since 1837, and traces the tropical adaptation of neoclassical architecture and the development of a native idiom. There are sixty-one major plates, illustrations of buildings prior to 1837, and a list of references.

397 **The Virgin Islands approach to housing and community development.**
Alonzo G. Moron. Charlotte Amalie, St. Thomas: Department of Housing and Community Renewal, 1965. 28p.
Moron's paper outlines the housing programme of the United States Virgin Islands with strategies and action plans. The paper was presented at the Urban Development Seminar in San Juan, Puerto Rico on 30 September 1965.

# Conservation

### 398   Anegada Reef protection plan.
Kenneth Clark.   *BVI Beacon*, vol. 5, no. 25 (1 Dec. 1988), p. 1, 4.
Clark reports on the Ministry of Natural Resources plan to designate Anegada
Horseshoe Reef as a fisheries protected area. This action resulted from a careful study
of United Nations findings in 1976, which confirmed that there are 185 species of fish
and 30 species of coral in the area.

### 399   Conservation Report, 1989.
Conservation Office.   Road Town, Tortola: British Virgin Islands
Government, 1990. 17p.
Summarizes the functions of the conservation office, its response to environmental
disasters, and projects started or completed during the year in review. The handling of
three major environmental disasters in the islands is described, as is the department's
method of monitoring natural environmental systems, a method which includes regular
studies of the beaches for the collection of specific data pertaining to the overmining of
sand or the nesting of leatherback turtles. We have here vital information from the first
report of an office newly established to review, plan, monitor, educate and enforce the
principles and spirit of the environment and conservation laws of the land.

### 400   Chief monuments of the British Virgin Islands.
David Buisseret, Barrie Clark.   In: *Report on chief monuments of
Antigua, the British Virgin Islands, the Cayman Islands, Dominica,
Grenada, Montserrat, St. Lucia, St. Vincent, the Turks and Caicos
Islands.*   London: British Development Division, p. 37-41.
For the most part, the monuments are military but a few great houses and ecclesiastical
remains are included in the descriptions. Details regarding the state of their current
condition are given along with recommendations for conserving those remains.

### 401   Island environments and development.
Christopher Howell, Edward Towle.   St. Thomas: Islands Resources
Foundation, 1976. maps.
A case-study which presents the potential for conserved development in the British
Virgin Islands. Several aspects of development are considered: economic, social,
cultural and environmental. The island is divided into a number of districts whose
conservational attributes are described. Colourful plans indicate the design of desirable
residential, business and recreational centres and there are several lists of buildings and
sites recommended for protective measures.

### 402   Sea Cow's Bay shorefront reclamation plan.
Ivor Jackson.   Road Town, Tortola: Town and Country Planning
Department, 1978. 5p. maps.
An action plan to redeem one of the southwestern bays lying alongside Drakes
Highway in the British Virgin Islands.

# Marine and wrecks

403   **An inventory of shipwrecks of the Virgin Islands, 1523-1825.**
Edward L. Towle, Robert Marx, Alan B. Albright.   St. Thomas:
Island Resources Foundation, 1976. 2nd rev. ed. 19p.

This very useful list of wrecks located mostly around the Horseshoe Reef of Anegada,
British Virgin Islands, was first published in mimeographed form in 1969. Towle relies
heavily on Lloyds List, a primary source, from which he culls sixty-five references.
Others come from Schomburgk's List, another primary source. The name, nationality,
tonnage, type of ship, date of sinking, and location are given.

404   **Four flakes of rust: a study of the Long Bay cannon, part one.**
D.A. Melford, G.R. Armstrong.   London: D.A. Melford, 1985. 35p.
maps.

Melford traces the origin and adventures of an ancient cast-iron cannon lying in Long
Bay, Tortola, British Virgin Islands. His search leads him to investigate the cannon's
design, the manner in which it was cast and he goes on to seek the ship that carried it.

405   **Four flakes revisited: a consideration of the Long Bay cannon, part two.**
D.A. Melford.   London: D.A. Melford, 1987. 17p. maps.

Following a further visit to the cannon, and more local research, the author revises
former conclusions and records them here. Both studies are significant for identifying
and preserving historical and marine artefacts.

406   **Ninety wrecks on Anegada, 1653-1843.**
D.A. Melford.   London: D.A. Melford, 1987. 30p. maps.

This fascinating and intriguing documentary accounts for the hundreds of disasters
which English, Spanish and American ships met when they encountered Anegada and
its associated system of coral reefs in the British Virgin Islands. Melford describes his
sources and points to gaps in other published works on the same topic. He includes
several important historical maps, for example, The Parliamentary map, 1823; Whittle
and Laurie's map, 1816; and Schomburgk's map, 1832.

# Virgin Islands, UK

407   **Management of coastal resources in the British Virgin Islands: plan of
operation.**
Castries, St. Lucia: Organization of Eastern Caribbean States, Natural
Resources Management Project, 1987. 17p. (vol. 8).

Based on an earlier workshop on 'Coastal zone management' held in 1986, this plan of
operation specifically addresses three objectives: 'Control of coastal development';
'Control of beach sand mining'; and 'Preservation of selected mangroves'. Each
objective is given a step-by-step action plan with inputs by manpower in number of
days and in total number of months, for the years 1987-90. This is a useful document
for monitoring coastal zone development on the islands.

**Discover nature's little secrets.**
*See* item no. 67.

**Tourism management, environmental and developmental issues.**
*See* item no. 79.

**Inter-Virgin Islands Conference.**
*See* item no. 253.

Marine reserve research reports.
*See* items no. 480-4.


# Virgin Islands, US

408 **A general review of sedimentation as it relates to environmental stress in the Virgin Islands biosphere and the Eastern Caribbean in general.**
Dennis Hubbard, Virgin Islands Resource Management Cooperative, Virgin Islands National Park.   St. Thomas: United States Department of the Interior National Park Service, West Indies Laboratory, Fairleigh Dickson University. 1987. 42p. maps. (Biosphere reserve report, no. 20).

Although this report also deals generally with the region, it is cited at this point because it deals very specifically with the United States Virgin Islands. Other reports in the series which examine the situation in St. John, United States Virgin Islands are also added here. They are: 'Sedimentation and reef development in Hawknest, Fish, and Reef bays, St. John, United States Virgin Islands' by Dennis Hubbard, Brian Carter and James Stump, Virgin Islands Resource Management Cooperative, Virgin Islands National Park, 1987. 99p. maps. (Biosphere reserve report, no. 21); and 'A basis for long term monitoring of fish and shellfish species in the Virgin Islands National Park' by Ralf H. Boulon, Virgin Islands Division of Fish and Wildlife, Department of Planning and Natural Resources, Virgin Islands National Park, 1987. 66p. maps. (Biosphere reserve report, no. 22).

409 **The Virgin Islands historic preservation grants manual.**
William Chapman.   Charlotte Amalie, St. Thomas: Division of Archaeology and Historic Preservation, Virgin Islands Planning Office, 1980.

The manual is divided into two main sections: Part 1 gives clear and precise instructions for making applications; and Part 2 gives instructions for completing projects. It is a useful guide for executives and fund-raisers working in the interests of conservation.

# Parks

## Virgin Islands, UK

410 **The Botanic Garden: a project.**
Road Town, Tortola: British Virgin Islands Botanic Society,
1985. 44p. map.
A captivating presentation of the British Virgin Islands Botanic Garden Project. It describes the historic garden site and the functions and aims of the Botanic Gardens. A plan of the gardens is provided as a fold-out map and there are illuminating descriptions of each of the following proposed sections: the J.R. O'Neal Centre; tea rooms and horticulturalist's flat; the pavilion; the lily-pond and bridge; the pergola walk; the cottage museum and produce garden; the rainforest garden; the palm, cycad and lily collection; the orchid collection; the jade vine gazebo; the bougainvillea gazebo; the fern house; the floral garden; the royal palm avenue; the succulent and cacti garden; the rare plant house; the medicinal or bush garden; the *Heliconia* collection; the seashore and dry bush collection; the *Ixora* collection; the *Bromeliad* collection; the bamboo and grass collection; the Christmas garden; the fountain and garden seats. All of this is charmingly illustrated by Margaret Barwick and Helen Lewis.

411 **Joseph Reynold O'Neal Botanic Gardens: British Virgin Islands.**
Road Town, Tortola: British Virgin Islands Botanic Society, 1991. 16p.
A progress report on the work of the Society for the years 1989 and 1990. There are listings of the executive and of the various categories of committee members, as well as the board of trustees and founder members. The report also assesses hurricane damage, activities, flower shows, financial support, plant sales and student awards.

412 **Parks and protected systems plan for the British Virgin Islands.**
Tighe Geoghegan, Allen Putney, Nicolas Clarke. Road Town,
Tortola: National Parks Trust and Eastern Caribbean Natural Area
Management Programme, 1986. 90p.
The report provides guidance for the development of an expanded system of parks and protected areas for the British Virgin Islands. The goal is to manage important natural areas in ways that will contribute to an improvement in the quality of life of the residents. The report suggests the positive impact an expanded system of parks would have on the tourist industry, the fisheries industry, the general progress of the economy; and the contributions it would make to education, scientific research, and to the conservation of endangered species and habitats.

413 **Gardens: underwater treasures.**
*Architecture Digest*, vol. 40 (Dec. 1983), p. 132-7.
This article illustrates the popular scuba-diving spots and underwater parks of the British Virgin Islands.

## Virgin Islands, US

414  **Cultural ambassadors in Virgin Islands National Park.**
Susan Vreeland.  *National Park*, vol. 57 (Sept.-Oct. 1983), p. 24-8.
Speaks of the valuable contribution of the work of tour-guide rangers Denise Georges
and Lito Valls as being an 'instructive, respectful, and tender experience for park
visitors', to the Virgin Islands National Park situated on St. John.

415  **Virgin Islands National Park, St. John Island, 'The quiet place.'**
Charles E. Hatch.   Washington, DC: National Park Service, 1972.
220p.
A detailed description of the National Park on St. John with special reference to
Annaberg Estate and Cinnamon Estate.

416  **Virgin Islands National Park.**
Alan Robinson.   Las Vegas, Nevada: NC Publications, 1974. 48p.
Robinson tells the behind-the-scenes story of the United States Virgin Islands National
Park: from the concept and unfolding of plans to finance and maintenance. It is
superbly illustrated in colour.

**Historic churches of the Virgin Islands.**
*See* item no. 191.

Marine reserve research reports.
*See* items 480-4.

**Fish and Wildlife News.**
*See* item no. 578.

**St. Croix Landmarks Society.**
*See* item no. 586.

# Environmental protection

417  **Survey of conservation priorities in the Lesser Antilles.**
Eastern Caribbean Natural Area Management Programme, Caribbean
Conservation Association.   Christiansted, St. Croix: University of
Michigan, School of Natural Resources, 1980. 26 vols. maps.
Each country in the group is dealt with in this survey. British Virgin Islands
information appears specifically under the titles: Anegada British Virgin Islands:
preliminary data atlas, 21p.; Virgin Gorda British Virgin Islands: preliminary data
atlas, 21p.; Tortola British Virgin Islands: preliminary data atlas, 21p. Topics
considered in each case are nature conservation, population density, resources
conservation, endangered species, national parks, nature reserves and land usage.
The final report of the survey was published in 1982 (37 pages). It covers general

conservation concerns in the Caribbean, such as ecosystems, endangered species, economic aspects, data collecting and data analysis.

418 **British Virgin Islands: harmonization of environmental legislation.**
Barbara Lausche. Castries, St. Lucia: Organization of Eastern
Caribbean States, Natural Resources Management Project, 1986. 48p.
(vol. 1).
A report which brings together and describes all national legislation on natural resources and related topics. It is the first stage in a project designed to revise and strengthen existing legislation.

419 **British Virgin Islands: harmonization of environmental legislation – plan
for updating legislation.**
Barbara Lausche. Castries, St. Lucia: Organization of Eastern
Caribbean States, Natural Resources Management Project, 1987. 20p.
(vol. 3).
Some of the priority areas listed for revision are: coastal resources conservation, nature conservation, control of recreational vessels, designation of restricted-use areas, beach development, and litter control.

420 **British Virgin Islands: harmonization of environmental legislation –
report and draft legislation for coastal conservation.**
Barbara Lausche. Castries, St. Lucia: Organization of Eastern
Caribbean States, Natural Resources Management Project, 1988. 27p.
(vol. 6).
Part one of this report highlights the main points of the draft and part two is the first draft of a coast conservation law. The text is preceded by a short title listing.

421 **British Virgin Islands: harmonization of environmental legislation –
report and draft legislation on protected areas and wildlife conservation.**
Barbara Lausche. Castries, St. Lucia: Organization of Eastern
Caribbean States, Natural Resources Management Project, 1988. 16p.
(vol. 7).
Section one is an analysis of the draft law, highlighting the purposes and the main points covered; section two represents the first draft of the protected areas and wildlife conservation.

422 **British Virgin Islands: management of coastal resources – programme
for sand mining control and management preservation.**
G. Chambers. Castries, St. Lucia: Organization of Eastern Caribbean
States, Natural Resources Management Project, 1987. 36p. (vol. 4).
Presents a plan of activities to control sand mining and to preserve mangroves in the British Virgin Islands. Special attention is devoted to Trellis Bay, Beef Island, and Josiah's Bay, Tortola, two abused areas.

423 **Marine environments of the Virgin Islands.**
St. Thomas: Islands Resources Foundation, 1977. 120p. maps.
Covering the sea, oceanography, habitats and aquatic environments, this survey describes and analyses each in its location.

424 **Virgin Islands bays: modelling of water gravity and pollution susceptibility.**
Maynard Nichols, Albert Kuo, Carl Cerco, Pamela Peebles.
Charlotte Amalie, St. Thomas: Division of Natural Resources Management and Islands Resources Foundation, 1979. 92p. maps.
The findings should have far-reaching effects for improving the quality of the environment and the quality of life in the area.

# Education

## General

425 **Educational development in Eastern Caribbean primary, secondary and tertiary levels.**
R.M. Nicholson. *Bulletin of Eastern Caribbean Affairs*, vol. 4, no. 3 (July-Aug. 1978), p. 24-8.
Nicholson scans and analyses a decade of educational progress in the region, from 1966 to 1977.

426 **Educational research: the English speaking Caribbean.**
Errol L. Miller. Ottawa, Canada: International Development Research Centre, 1984. 199p.
This is a vital tool for keeping abreast with what educational research has been done in the region.

427 **Food and nutrition education: a guide for college tutors in the English-speaking Caribbean.**
Kingston, Jamaica: Caribbean Food and Nutrition Institute, 1987. 182p.
This is a long-awaited general guide to constructing syllabuses for a vital section of the curriculum. There are many tables and illustrations.

428 **The primary education project.**
Leonard Shorey. *Bulletin of Eastern Caribbean Affairs*, vol. 7, no. 3 (July-Aug. 1981), p. 22-5.
The University of the West Indies' coordinator of the four-year project (1980-84) – funded by the US Agency for International Development in the Eastern Caribbean and Jamaica – states the project's objective as: 'to enhance primary school education

and the quality of administration and educational planning by concentrating on five schools in each territory in three of the following subject areas: language, arts, maths, science and social studies'. Implementation and evaluation officers, including four specialists in subject areas, were appointed in each island. Resource materials were to be produced and a series of workshops were scheduled to be conducted at territorial and regional levels. Shorey was satisfied with the initial success and he envisaged benefits spiralling to non-project schools as well. The British Virgin Islands schools participated in the project.

429 **Report on the University of the West Indies Distance Teaching Experiment.**
Gerald C. Lalor, Christine Marrett.   Mona, Jamaica: UWI, 1986. 84p.
This report describes the teaching materials and methods, programmes, costs, future development and the response to the distance teaching experiment. The authors assess the model as one which smaller countries could use to introduce various categories of their communities to the power of modern telecommunication and to a new learning option.

430 **Teaching and testing for excellence: an address.**
Roy Marshall.   Bridgetown, Barbados: Caribbean Examination Council, 1988. 10p.
This address touches on a wide range of educational topics: examinations, qualifications, teaching and training, curriculum subjects; courses, teaching methods and teaching personnel. It was given at the annual awards presentation of the Caribbean Examinations Council in Barbados on 7 October 1988. Secondary education in all British Caribbean countries, including the British Virgin Islands, is assessed by the Caribbean Examination Council and this address, upholding some of the aspirations of the Council, is both inspiring and informative for educators across the Caribbean region.

# Virgin Islands, UK

431 **British Virgin Islands salutes Caribbean Examinations Council (CXC).**
Department of Education and Culture.   Road Town, Tortola: Ministry of Health, Education and Welfare, 1988. 32p.
A fitting congratulatory issue for the fifteenth anniversary of the Caribbean Examination Council. Specific achievements in curriculum building, teaching and training programmes and the general strengthening of educational systems during the years in review are highlighted in articles, messages and poetry. British Virgin Islands candidates and subjects are listed for 1979-88.

432 **Comprehension for Caribbean examinations: multi-choice and other exercises.**
J. Wheatley, T.B. Parris, C.H. Wheatley. London: Macmillan Caribbean, 1979. 118p.

A useful book for fourth- and fifth-year students in secondary schools, preparing for the Caribbean Examination Council and GCE examinations. It consists of a wide variety of stimulus materials including prose, poetry, plays, cartoons, advertisements and maps from the West Indies and elsewhere. There are suggestions for research and further reading. The authors are educators in the British Virgin Islands.

433 **Development through the performing arts.**
Road Town, Tortola: Department of Education and Culture, 1985.

The theme for Education Week, 10-17 March 1985, inspired a collection of folktales, poems, dances and games. The concert programme of traditional and non-traditional musical items performed during the week is also recorded.

434 **Education: Dominica, Bermuda, St. Kitts, Montserrat, Cayman Islands, British Virgin Islands, Turks and Caicos Islands.**
Census Research Programme. Kingston, Jamaica: University of the West Indies, CCRS, CIDA, [n.d.]. 359p.

Volume 6, part 3 is devoted to educational statistics of the islands named in the title, including the British Virgin Islands.

435 **Education in the British Virgin Islands.**
Norwell Harrigan. In: *Leewards: writings, past and present about the Leeward Islands.* [n.p.], Barbados: Department of Extra Mural Studies, 1961, p. 18-23.

This is a critical look at the development of education in the islands; the strengths, virtues and weaknesses inherited from various influences are pinpointed but the author also unveils a vision for the future.

436 **Education report for the year 1989/90.**
Road Town, Tortola: Department of Education and Culture, 1990. 76p.

An up-to-date source of information about education in the territory. It describes the general education system; outstanding developments; weaknesses and resolutions. There are also useful comparative statistics on enrolment, staff, local and Caribbean examinations, and on expenditures.

437 **Education in the British Virgin Islands: a small country case study.**
Charles R.D. Smawfield. PhD thesis, University of Hull, 1988. 393p. bibliog.

This thesis examines education in the British Virgin Islands. The author selects themes and issues such as: 'the teaching force and its training with particular reference to 1950-85; the 1986-89 Hull University teacher education programmes in the British Virgin Islands; the provision of vocational and tertiary education; and "a small country" interpretation of education'. In his conclusion, he outlines the establishing of a 'small country' perspective and its application to the British Virgin Islands case.

438 **Educational development project of the Governments of the Eastern Caribbean through the United Nations Development Programme.**
Alfred Sangster. Kingston, Jamaica: College of Arts, Science and Technology, 1986. 46p. maps.
This is a preliminary assessment and proposals for the future development of a multi-island educational development project. The British Virgin Islands was one of the selected testing areas.

439 **Innovation in the high school curriculum on a micro-scale.**
Quincey Lettsome. MEd thesis, University of Manchester, 1977. 105, 26p. maps.
This work examines the following areas: the inadequacies and irrelevance of the secondary education system introduced from England; the Commonwealth West Indies with specific reference to the British Virgin Islands; colonial secondary education in islands communities and micro-states; the present high-school curriculum of the British Virgin Islands; trends, possibilities and barriers. The author concludes that 'the most crucial factor is the political nature of curriculum development and therefore its implementation will depend on a political decision'.

440 **Learning from the environment.**
Road Town, Tortola: Department of Education and Culture, 1988. 54p.
This souvenir booklet contains descriptive articles about the land, the sea and the natural wonders of the islands. It was written by students and teachers throughout the territory for Education Week, 13-20 March 1988.

441 **Literacy for all: our focus for the decade.**
Road Town, Tortola: Department of Education and Culture, 1990. 68p.
This illustrated booklet, commemorating Education Week, 11-18 March 1990, contains urgent messages and articles from officials, educators, local writers and students, on a crucially important theme.

442 **Nutrition lesson plans – supplement to food and nutrition education in the primary school: a handbook for Caribbean teachers.**
Patricia Isaacs, Doris Bamble, Versada Campbell. Kingston, Jamaica: Caribbean Food and Nutrition Institute, 1987. 169p.
This well-illustrated guide is a useful tool for Caribbean education departments and teachers who wish to make the curricula more appropriate and meaningful.

443 **The preservation of culture through education.**
Road Town, Tortola: Department of Education and Culture, 1983.
64p.
A collection of articles by teachers and a wide range of creative work by students, produced for Education Week, 13-18 March 1983.

444 **Report of the survey team on secondary education in the British Virgin Islands.**
M.K. Bacchus. Road Town, Tortola: British Virgin Islands Government, 1976. 88p.
The report surveys existing provision for secondary education in the British Virgin Islands, taking into account population projections; teacher supply; funding; timetabling; levels; facilities; the Lavender–Saunders report of 1969, the Elkan–Morley report of 1970, and appropriate reports of the Education Department. A total of twenty-five recommendations are recorded, relating to the administrative structure; teacher training; school discipline; introduction of a technical and vocational programme; the appointment of a guidance officer; reviving the presence of the University of the West Indies in the territory; and to the field of primary education.

445 **School plan: 'self-sufficiency.'**
Chris Bergeron. *British Virgin Island Beacon*, vol. 7, no. 38 (14 March 1991), p. 1, 9.
The Virgin Islands' first five-year education development plan is announced in this report. It promises to enhance 'the learning environment by providing school buildings and equipment appropriate for learning in the 21st century . . . and secure training for teachers . . . in order that they may deliver required services'. The plan emphasizes 'participatory approaches and programmes', and it recognizes the importance of incorporating elements of traditional culture in the educational process. Another fundamental aim of the plan is to 'broaden the scope of basic education' for remedial students, slow learners and the handicapped. The report includes comment from government ministers and from the chief education officer.

446 **Teacher education in the Virgin Islands.**
Pearl Varlack. PhD thesis, Pittsburgh University, 1974. 169p. bibliog.
This pioneering work formulates strategic propositions for teacher education and curriculum design. It presents a theoretical overview, the socio-eco milieu, the existing education system and a series of seventeen propositions suited to the needs of the Virgin Islands society. The author is a professor of Education at the University of the Virgin Islands. (The thesis is available from University Microfilms, Ann Arbor, Michigan.)

447 **Setting up a family-life education programme for the British Virgin Islands.**
Doris Farrington Hepburn. MEd thesis, University of Phoenix, Rio Piedras, Puerto Rico, 1984. 140p. bibliog.
The author's stated purposes in this study are: to determine if students of the British Virgin Islands are receiving adequate information on family-life education; from what sources; how this is affecting their overall attitude to their own sexuality, peers, work

and responsibility; and to find out the overall attitude of students, teachers and parents to having a Family-Life Education Programme as part of the school curriculum. Thirty tables are included. (The University of Phoenix has a residence centre in Puerto Rico.)

448 **Virgin Islands Secondary School: Silver Jubilee, 1943-1968.**
Edited by Adorothy Turnbull. Road Town, Tortola: Jubilee Committee, 1969. 144p.

This memento was planned to portray, in words and pictures, the entire twenty-five years of the secondary school. There are lists of staff and students, reminiscences and photographs.

449 **Official renaming of the Long Look Primary School, Wednesday 2 November 1988.**
Road Town, Tortola: Department of Education and Culture, 1988. 11p.

This booklet records the history of Long Look School and its former principals. It includes a chronology, a biographical sketch of Francis Lettsome, one of the benefactors, and the programme of items which took place on the day of the renaming ceremony.

450 **Reading: our goal for all.**
Edited by Patricia Turnbull. Road Town, Tortola: Education Department, 1987. 79p.

The souvenir magazine commemorating Education Week, 8-15 March 1987. It contains useful articles by professionals and specialists on the progress and future of reading and educational development in the territory, such as: 'Setting up a reading programme' by language specialist, Medita Malone, p. 11-15; 'Teaching remedial reading' by Kirlin Lettsome, p. 22-3; 'The university and the community' by Colin Brock, p. 24-5; 'Libraries for all' by Peter Moll, p. 28-9; and 'Reading: the need in our prison' by Calvin Hodge, p. 36-7. The publication's assistant editors were Joseph Harrigan, Jennie Wheatley, Esmeralda O'Neal, Lynden Smith, Edith Dotson, Eileen Parsons and Elvin Stoutt. Messages from Government ministers and examples of creative writing and drawings by young pupils are also included.

451 **Teachers learn more about deadly syndrome.**
*Island Sun*, no. 1610 (13 April 1991), p. 1-2.

The report of a three-day workshop on 'AIDS education in schools', in which twenty teachers were oriented into the teaching of the HIV infection and AIDS curriculum. They also discussed social and public health issues raised by AIDS and HIV infection. The workshop was sponsored by the PAHO (Pan American Health Organization) and the Ministry of Health, Education and Welfare on 8 May 1991.

# Students and organizations

452 **British Virgin Islands students abroad.**
Chief Minister's Office.    Road Town, Tortola: British Virgin Islands
Government, 1976. 8p.
This guide is updated periodically and indicates students' names, courses studied,
length of course, name of university and by whom funded.

453 **List of scholarships, training awards and student loans available.**
Chief Minister's Office.    Road Town, Tortola: British Virgin Islands
Government, 1976. 14p.
Especially valuable to career guidance officers, high-school students in their final year
and also to mature students who may wish to improve their skills and qualifications.
Lists are published periodically. Although this one is dated, the information is
useful for retrospective study.

454 **British Virgin Islands Scout Association: fifty years of service.**
Edited by Dancia Penn, Valentine Lewis, Jennie Wheatley, illustrated
by Bryan Chick.    British Virgin Islands Scout Association, 1982. 30p.
The story of the Scout movement in the British Virgin Islands from 1932 to 1982 is
recorded, with illustrations, photographs, messages and articles.

# Higher education

455 **British Virgin Islands Community College.**
Road Town, Tortola: Board of Governors, 1990. 24p.
The prospectus of the newly founded Community College of the British Virgin Islands.
It contains the mission statement; lists of governors, staff and committees; a general
plan of courses; description of individual courses; and information on registration,
transcripts and fees.

456 **The development of secondary and tertiary education for microstates.**
Quincey Filmore V. Lettsome.    PhD thesis, Universities of Hull,
Newcastle, Manchester, 1990. 515p. bibliog.
Lettsome organizes his work in four main parts: 'A résumé of the Commonwealth
Caribbean context; The development of education in the anglophone Caribbean with
special reference to secondary and tertiary sectors; Microstates: case studies and
comparative comment; and An innovation model based on the British Virgin Islands.
In chapter twelve, he discloses how the plan should be implemented.

457 **Higher education in a micro-state: a theory of the Raran society.**
Norwell E. Harrigan. PhD thesis, Pittsburgh University, 1972. 189p.
bibliog. (Available from University Microfilms, Ann Arbor, Michigan).
The study traces the socio-economic development of the Virgin Islands in historic
terms; contrasts the main characteristics of developed and developing countries and
attempts to build a model of Raran society; draws a profile of an institution of higher
education appropriate to the particular needs of Raran society. It also examines critical
issues of higher education in current world situations and the place of higher education
in Raran society. The author, an eminent Caribbean educator, was director of the
Caribbean Research Institute and has written several books and articles on Virgin
Island concerns.

458 **Local University of the West Indies centre planned.**
*Island Sun*, no. 1603 (23 Feb. 1991), p. 13.
According to this report, a University of the West Indies centre for continuing studies,
is to be established on the campus of the Community College in the British Virgin
Islands by mid-1991. Initially, the British Virgin Islands government will provide
accommodation and salary for the resident tutor while the University of the West
Indies will provide the apparatus for the distance-learning system.

**British Virgin Islands: territorial report for the year 1987.**
*See* item no. 9.

**A history of the British Virgin Islands, 1672 to 1970.**
*See* item no. 122.

**The Virgin Islands story.**
*See* item no. 126.

**Methodism: two hundred years in the British Virgin Islands.**
*See* item no. 188.

**Tortola: a Quaker experiment of long ago in the tropics.**
*See* item no. 189.

**Basic sea skills course.**
*See* item no. 533.

# Virgin Islands, US

459 **Black education in the Danish West Indies from 1732-1853.**
Eva Lawaetz, prefaced by Dr Robert V. Vaughn. St. Croix: St. Croix
Friends of Denmark Society, 1980. 90p. bibliog.
This important study of the pioneering efforts of the Moravian Brethren, reveals many
early problems in establishing a system of education in the Virgin Islands, viz.,
problems created by languages – the Danish official language, the English language of

the gentry, German as a trade language, African and Creole languages. There are useful appendixes and a chronology.

460   **Help them become their best through education that is multicultural.**
Yegin Habteyes, edited by Lois Latifah Chinnery.   St. Thomas: Virgin Islands Teachers Corps Project, 1978. 102p.

This work focuses on the implication of the 1978 Teacher Corps' mandate which required objectives specifying education that is multicultural at both national and local levels. Appendixes A and B list proverbs from Africa and African games. The certification and registration requirements for educational institutions appear as Virgin Islands Rules and Regulations, Title 17, Chapter 10.

461   **Parents' handbook.**
Foreword by Ruth Thomas.   Charlotte Amalie, St. Thomas: Charlotte Amalie High School assisted by Department of Education, 1979. 12p.

Intended to communicate with parents, this handbook explains the history of the school, its heraldry, publications, administration, uniform, classification of students and identification cards. There is also detailed information about textbooks, attendance, study programmes, the grading system, report cards, guidance services, health services, library services, graduation requirements, honours graduates and transcripts. Written in simple language and comprehensive in coverage, this is a model communicative tool. Another more recent work by Ruth Thomas is *We must focus on our youth* (*Virgin Islands Daily News*, 21 Oct. 1991, p.1). In this guest editorial she says that 'education should result in changes of attitude and behaviour . . . and students must know at all times and in all places what is expected of them.' The article challenges government and community to 'keep the students in full view' when planning educational environments but it also expects a positive response from students. A former Charlotte Amalie High School principal, the writer conducts seminars and workshops, lectures on challenging topics throughout the islands and presents a weekly current affairs radio programme. She is a University of the Virgin Islands trustee and serves as an examiner in foreign languages for Cambridge University, England.

462   **Programme aims at the academically talented.**
Judith Williams.   *Pride*, vol. 8, no. 12 (Dec. 1989), p. 11.

An encouraging article on the current status of the programme (for the gifted and talented) which was established within the public school system in 1978.

463   **The Virgin Islands: a comprehensive survey completed at the request of the commissioner of education.**
Centre for School Services.   New York: School of Education, 1962. [var. pag.].

The document provides a retrospective survey of education in the United States Virgin Islands.

464   **Virgin Islands Montessori School.**
St. Thomas: Montessori School, 1960.

Provides a retrospective look at one of the islands' private schools. The school also currently issues handbooks and newsletters annually.

465  **Virgin Islands of the United States public school basic skills achievement survey: Technical report no. 1.**
Leonard B. Bliss.   St. Thomas: Caribbean Research Institute, 1982.
46p.
This first report deals with validation of the use of the Stanford Achievement Test with United States Virgin Islands children. It is clearly set out with illustrations and figures.

# Higher education

466  **University of the Virgin Islands.**
In: *World of learning, 1991.*   London: Europa Publications, 1990.
p. 1825.
The University, situated in St. Thomas in the United States Virgin Islands, with a branch on St. Croix, is described as 'a four-year liberal arts college with professional programmes'. The address, the year of its foundation, names of executive staff, and the numbers of teachers, students and library volumes are given.

467  **Virgin Islands adult and continuing education programme.**
Charlotte Amalie, St. Thomas: Department of Education, 1977. 11p.
This useful and popular guide to courses available in adult education was reprinted in 1979 with additional subjects and classes.

**A history of the Virgin Islands of the United States.**
*See* item no. 130.

**Virgin Islands story: a history of the Lutheran State Church . . . education and culture in the Danish West Indies, now the Virgin Islands.**
*See* item no. 196.

**Discover the arts in the United States Virgin Islands.**
*See* item no. 490.

**Social Sciences Newsletter.**
*See* item no. 584.

**Virgin Islands Education Review.**
*See* item no. 590.

# Human Resources
# Development

468  **A calendar of local and international seminars, conferences and self-development programmes.**
Kingston, Jamaica: Department of Library Studies, University of the West Indies, 1989. 26p.
A useful guide to on-going learning opportunities available in the region and in the wider world. These would enhance in-service training programmes, especially for technical and semi-professional staff.

469  **Communication.**
Mitchelle Abbott-Smith.  *Island Sun* (6 Jan. 1990), p. 13. (The Communicator series).
Abbott-Smith deals with a wide range of communication topics in the series which this item introduces. The series is well presented, with crisp definitions and clear explanations. Topics include: 'What is communication?'; 'Why communication is important to business'; 'Creativity and the communication process'; 'Thinking of starting a business?'; 'Identifying the mass media'. The writer is the director of Aaronsrod, a business communication firm.

470  **Lyons guide to the career jungle.**
Laura Lyons.  Dallas, Texas: Odenwald Press, 1989. 85p. bibliog.
This small volume includes material from the author's lectures to various groups in government and private sectors throughout both groups of islands. It touches on loyalty, peer pressure, politics, positive mental attitude, problem solving, productivity and visibility in the workplace. Lyons also lectures throughout the Caribbean and even as far afield as South Africa.

# Science and Technology

471 **Blueprint for paradise: how to live on a tropical island.**
Ross Norgrove.    Camden, Maine: International Publishing, 1983.
209p. 3 maps.

A useful manual which provides guidance, practical advice and plans for building a house on a tropical island. The author has first-hand experience of many island groups, from Fiji to the Bahamas, and various anecdotes illustrating folk-life make the contents realistic and interesting. The composite Virgin group is covered but the British Virgin Islands more extensively so, as Norgrove and his wife have made their home there. Appropriate illustrations include professional colour plates which highlight the tropical island scenery. Useful appendixes include: further recommended reading; a record of revolving storms; the addresses of the manufacturers of prefabricated houses; and resources. Place-names referred to in the index are identified by the name of the island group in parenthesis.

472 **Cyclones: improving building construction procedures in the Caribbean.**
A.T. Watson.    St. Johns, Antigua: Pan-Caribbean Disaster
Preparedness Programme, 1985. 32p.

This is one in a series of building guides which had to be formulated as a result of the destruction wrought by recent hurricanes in the region. It is an easy step-by-step handbook showing proportions and percentages for reinforcing building construction.

473 **Renewable energy trends and opportunities in the Caribbean.**
Wallace C. Koehler.    St. Johns, Antigua: Centre for Energy and
Environment Research, 1983. 17p.

Contains useful findings for discussion at national, regional and international levels. It was actually prepared for discussion at the joint meeting of the Human Settlements and Economic Affairs Secretariat of the Organization of Eastern Caribbean States (OECS).

474 **Boat launchings in changing times.**
Dean Greenaway. *BVI Beacon*, vol. 6, no. 1 (8 June 1980), p. 18.

The launching of a twenty-foot boat, the *Effort*, in the village of East End, Tortola, is illustrated with photographs and text that convey the voices of the sea captains of former generations. It compares launchings then with now, and notes how times have changed.

475 **Energy Survey Report.**
Bridgetown, Barbados: Caribbean Development Bank, 1986.

A detailed energy audit of several hotels in the British Virgin Islands. The visits to the hotels to collect data were made during December 1985. Current energy systems and their energy use were compared with historical energy use patterns and occupancy rates. The report offers recommendations but emphasizes that measurements taken over a longer time-span would provide a more adequate picture of use trends. It concludes that energy costs could be reduced through a coordinated effort of management staff, a good working plan, and an accurate system of recording and monitoring energy use. The hotels surveyed on Tortola were: The Moorings, Castle Maria, Prospect Reef, Treasure Island; and on Virgin Gorda: Fisher's Cove, Trade Winds Resort, and Biras Creek.

476 **Recycling scrap metals.**
Chris Bergeron. *BVI Beacon*, vol. 7, no. 36 (28 Feb. 1991), p. 8.

Reveals the enthusiasm of recyclers Mike Masters and Robert Richardson who hope to turn their commitment to the environment into a profitable business. The company, Mike Masters Magic Metals, purchases scrap metal – copper, bronze and aluminum – crushes it in a metal crusher and ships it to Puerto Rico where a metal company buys it. According to the report, Mike Masters is also investigating other redeemable scrap, such as beer bottles and glass for road making. His aim is to show 'how recycling can be a profitable way to preserve the scenic beauty of the British Virgin Islands'.

477 **The Tortola boat characteristics: origin and demise.**
Edwin Doran. *Supplement to the Mariner's Mirror*, vol. 56, no. 1 (1970). 61p. bibliog.

This study, which is the result of earlier research in 1964 and fieldwork carried out in 1966, is a significant contribution to the preservation of the local craft. It outlines the historical development of the native sloop in the islands and gives many details of building proportions and about the skills of the islands' shipwrights. Many tables, illustrations and plates assist in highlighting the craft's 'distinctive features' which include: 'the beam is equal to half the length of the keel; the stern-post, one third the keel; the mast, twice the keel; the boom, the keel plus the stern-post'. There are several photographs of historical sloops, vessels and famous local shipwrights.

478 **The Virgin Islands Energy Office: who we are and what we do.**
Janet A. Crawford. Frederiksted, St. Croix: Virgin Islands Energy Office, 1983. 17p.

The functions and activities of the Energy Office are cleverly presented with many illustrations.

# Scientific Institutions
# and Research

479 **Caribbean Research Institute.**
Edited by Clara Lewis, Liz Wilson, foreword by Arthur Richards.
Charlotte Amalie, St. Thomas: Caribbean Research Institute,
University of the Virgin Islands, [n.d.]. 24p.
An illustrated description of the work of the Institute, its functions, objectives and
programmes. The overall aim, says D.S. Padda, the Vice-President, 'is to develop and
disseminate social and technical knowledge to protect fragile environments and
enhance the quality of life in the Virgin Islands'. Four activity centres which help the
Institute to achieve its goal are: Social Research Centre, Water Resources Research
Centre, Environmental Research Centre and the Ecological Research Centre. Each
centre is fully described; there is a directory of the Institute's staff and a listing of its
publications up to 1987. Although the document is not for sale it is of significant
importance and is available for reference in libraries.

480 **Marine community descriptions and maps within the Virgin Islands
National Park biosphere reserve.**
James Beets, Lance Lewand, Caribbean Research Institute, Virgin
Islands National Park. St. Thomas: Virgin Islands Resource
Management Cooperative, 1985. 118p. maps. (Biosphere reserve
research report, no. 2).
This is a mini-encyclopaedia on marine organisms and their sites within the National
Parks system. This whole series is a massive collaboration of research effort,
concentrating on the ecology and geology of both groups of Virgin Islands.
Descriptions, analyses and recommendations are expertly presented with the aid of
many maps, illustrations and tables. Various authors and publishers have contributed.
Those reports in which author or publisher is identical are grouped in one annotation,
for example: 'Collection of common organisms within the Virgin Islands National Park
biosphere reserve', 1985. 45p. maps (Biosphere reserve research report, no. 3).

481 **Ecological community type maps and biological community, descriptions of Buck Island Reef National Park Monument and proposed marine sites in the British Virgin Islands.**
Miles Anderson, Holly Lund, Elizabeth Gladfelter, Mike Davis, Virgin Islands Resource Management Cooperative, Virgin Islands National Park. St. Thomas: US Department of Interior National Park Service, 1986. [n.p.]. maps. (Biosphere reserve research report, no. 4).

An important document containing the necessary findings to enhance efforts for the protection of Buck Island reef. The latter is of great cultural and environmental value to the British Virgin Islands. Other works by the same authors include: 'Trends in recreational boating in the British Virgin Islands', US Department of Interior National Park Service, West Indies Laboratory, Fairleigh Dickenson University, 1986. 40p. maps (Biosphere reserve research report, no. 3); 'A preliminary assessment of a monitoring programme for safe anchorages' (Biosphere reserve research report, no. 5); 'Geographic range and research plan for monitoring white band disease'. 1986. 28p. maps (Biosphere reserve research report, no. 6); 'Marine ecosystems of the Lesser Antilles: identification of representative sites'. 1986. 44p. maps (Biosphere reserve research report, no. 7).

482 **Data synthesis and development of a basis for zoning of the Virgin Islands.**
Allen Putney, Eastern Caribbean Natural Area Management Programme. St. Thomas: US Department of Interior National Park Service, West Indies Laboratory, Fairleigh Dickenson University, 1987. 44p. maps. (Biosphere reserve research report, no. 15).

A valid piece of documentation which brings together the accessible data needed to assess the zoning needs of the Virgin Islands. 'Conceptual framework of the management of the Virgin Islands biosphere reserve' is another in the series by the Virgin Islands Resource Management Cooperative, Virgin Islands National Park and published in St. Thomas by US Department of the Interior National Park Service, Eastern Caribbean Natural Area Management Programme, 1987. 21p. (Biosphere reserve research report, no. 16).

483 **Herbarium of the Virgin Islands National Park.**
Walter I. Knausenberger, John M. Matuszak, Toni Ackerman, Virgin Islands Resource Management Cooperative, Virgin Islands National Park. St. Thomas: US Department of the Interior National Park Service, University of the Virgin Islands Extension Service, 1987. 51p. (Biosphere reserve research report, no. 18A).

Describes the consolidatory work and curation of a reference collection of indigenous herbs. Another report on which two of the above authors worked is: 'Establishment and soil characterization of long-term forest monitoring plots in the Virgin Islands biosphere reserve' by John M. Matuszak, Ellen Craft and Walter I. Knausenberger, Virgin Islands Resource Management Cooperative, Virgin Islands National Park, 1987. 81p. maps (Biosphere reserve research report, no. 18B).

484 **Initiation of a long-term monitoring programme for coral reefs in the Virgin Islands National Park.**
Caroline Rogers, Evonne Zullo, Virgin Islands Resource Management Cooperative, Virgin Islands National Park. St. Thomas: US Department of the Interior National Park Service, 1987. 33p. maps. (Biosphere reserve research report, no. 17).

The reefs are listed by location and a plan for ensuring their protection is outlined. Another report in the series is: 'Historic land use in the Reef Bay, Fish Bay, and Hawksnest Bay watersheds, St. John, United States Virgin Islands 1718-1950' by George F. Tyson Jr, Virgin Islands Resource Management Cooperative, Virgin Islands National Park, 1987. 54p. maps (Biosphere reserve research report, no. 19).

# Culture and the Arts

## Culture

### Virgin Islands, UK

485 **Our ancestral heritage: a bibliography of the roots of culture in the English-speaking Caribbean.**
Compiled by Edward Braithwaite.   Kingston, Jamaica: Savacou, 1977. 194p.

Specially prepared for Carifesta, the Caribbean Festival of Arts of 1976, this work guides the reader through the general background of the Caribbean, its peoples, European settlements, the plantation era and the impact of all these influences. The British Virgin Islands participated in the Festival.

486 **British Virgin Islands Festival, 1989.**
British Virgin Islands Festival Committee (Chairman: Ishmael Scatliffe), with an editorial by Reginald Penn.   Road Town, Tortola: Neil Blyden Associates, 1989. 20p.

The cover of this booklet shows colourful, happy individuals jumping to the rhythm of calypso music. It records the theme of the 1989 festival as 'Let freedom shine in '89', and it celebrates the abolition of slavery in the British Virgin Islands in 1834. The schedule of events for Festival Week is listed and includes: 'Opening ceremonies and entertainment'; 'Teenagers' Night'; 'Family Evening'; 'Festival Fashions'; 'Salute to Reggae Music'; 'Costume Presentation'; 'Calypsonians' Night'; 'Dancers' Showcase'; 'Food, Arts and Crafts Exhibition'; 'Emancipation Thanksgiving and Festival Queen Show'; 'August Monday Parade'; 'Aquatic Sports and Horse Racing'. The Chairman's message is forceful: '. . . today we celebrate our freedom from man's inhumanity to man . . . but all is not well in the world and some people are still suffering from oppression, inhumanity, war and poverty'.

487 **Christmas in the Virgin Islands.**
Ermin Burnett.    East End, Tortola: E.& R. Burnett, 1983. 36p.
This vividly illustrated booklet attempts to record Christmas as it was traditionally celebrated in the British Virgin Islands, and as a child would have experienced it in the 1950s and early 1960s. It includes recipes for some typical local foods and the text is executed in a distinctive cursive style.

488 **Crafts alive.**
*News Release*, 9 9R/91 (17 May 1990), p. 1-2.
The British Virgin Islands Trade Department is organizing a summer fair and exposition to augment the August festival activities. The market will feature locally made and designed hats, dolls, pottery; savoury sauces, sweetmeats, tarts, jellies; fungi and steel bands; and more work by local artists, all designed to give a truer reflection of the local culture.

489 **National cultural policy for the British Virgin Islands: report and recommendations.**
A.J. Seymour.    Road Town, Tortola: UNESCO for the British Virgin Islands Government, 1981. 27p.
The report assesses the plans of the Government of the British Virgin Islands for cultural development and makes recommendations in order that a framework for a National Cultural Policy may be devised. It is a useful document which defines culture, discusses the aims and principles of a cultural policy, examines the literary and folk arts traditions and scans the efforts of existing cultural institutions. Appendixes included are: family names in British Virgin Islands history; officials and private individuals consulted; books consulted; and the background of the consultant who conducted the survey.

**The beautiful British Virgin Islands.**
*See* item no. 8.

**Tourism and perspectives of cultural change on Virgin Gorda: patterns and processes.**
*See* item no. 77.

**The Virgin Islands story.**
*See* item no. 126.

**The folklore of the British Virgin Islands.**
*See* item no. 179.

**Afro-Caribbean folk medicine.**
*See* items no. 212.

**Cane Garden Bay.**
*See* item no. 386.

**Culture and the Arts.** Culture

**Landscapes of the past.**
*See* item no. 394.

**Boat launchings in changing times.**
*See* item no. 474.

**The Tortola boat characteristics: origin and demise.**
*See* item no. 477.

# Virgin Islands, US

490 **Discover the arts in the United States Virgin Islands.**
Ruth Moore. St. Croix: Virgin Islands Council on the Arts, National
Endowment for the Arts, 1985. 83p.
This work describes art organizations in the islands, giving a brief history, date
founded, the function and objectives of each. It further 'attempts to turn the resident
and visitor alike to the views beyond the surface beauty of the islands, to that which
makes human activity joyous and beautiful in itself'. The book is profusely illustrated
with photographs, motifs and drawings.

491 **The living arts and crafts of the West Indies.**
Florence Lewisohn, Walter Lewisohn, illustrated by Barbara
Meadows. Christiansted, St. Croix: Virgin Islands Council of the Arts
and the National Endowment for the Arts in Washington, DC, 1973.
56p.
Barbara Meadows's sketches of original Caribbean cultural objects range from
religious art, paintings, daily life, musicians and dancers, to woven crafts and children's
toys. The book was designed to encourage greater interest in the arts and crafts of the
entire West Indies and to preserve those already existing. It represents the
fundamental aspects of the Council, viz., the collection and study of materials; the
creation of museum exhibits in the Virgin Islands; the establishment of demonstration
areas where visitors may watch skilled artisans working; and the development of arts
and crafts through island shops.

492 **The Virgin Islands Carnival book.**
Charlotte Amalie, St. Thomas: Virgin Islands Carnival Committee,
1951. [var. pag.].
Issued annually in conjunction with St. Thomas carnival, the title of this publication
varies, but it is usually an illustrated bulletin of the carnival, listing carnival
committees, floats, bands, and the processional order of the street parade.

493 **Virgin Islands Christmas-time.**
St. Thomas: Department of Education, [n.d.]. [n.p.]. bibliog. (Project
Introspection).
This work is Title 111 in the ESEA series. The illustrations, songs and musical scores
complement the description of Christmas customs in the islands.

146

494   **The Virgin Islands international film festival and film market.**
Charlotte Amalie, St. Thomas: Virgin Islands International Film
Festival Ltd, 1975. [n.p.].
The book of programmes for the film festival held on 7-16 November 1975. There is a
handy index of the films which were shown. The festival is held periodically only, and
this first programme will remain a reference source for future programming.

**Afro-Caribbean villages in historical perspective.**
*See* item no. 149.

**Afro-Caribbean folk medicine.**
*See* item no. 212.

**Cultural aspects of delusion: a psychiatric study of the Virgin Islands.**
*See* items no. 226.

**St. Croix Landmarks Society.**
*See* item no. 586.

# The arts

## Virgin Islands, UK

495   **Virgin Island sketches.**
Roger Burnett.   Road Town, Tortola: The author, 1985. 2nd. ed. 64p.
map.
A varied collection of pen-and-ink drawings of 'everyday things' which capture the
islands' history and culture. Historic buildings and local architecture, plantation
houses, churches, forts, distilleries, boatbuilding and backyard scenes, are all recorded.
Descriptive notes set each drawing or series of drawings in their respective historical or
cultural context, making this art collection a permanent gallery for anyone interested in
the islands to wander through and enjoy. The artist has been painting Caribbean
scenes since 1985.

496   **A taste of guavaberry: a collection of songs.**
Quincey Lettsome.   Road Town, Tortola: British Virgin Islands
Teachers Union, 1984. [n.p.].
Lettsome has extended his enthusiasm for creating collections of poetry to collecting
popular local songs. 'Ah cum for me guavaberry', a favourite especially at Christmas-
time, is the most popular among them. The foreword is by Marilyn Dickson, Executive
Assistant of the Federation of Women Teachers' Associations of Ontario, Canada.

497 **Creative arts in the British Virgin Islands: a festival.**
Edited by Verna Penn. Road Town, Tortola: Virgin Islands Public
Library, 1979. 32p.

The revival of cultural interest in the islands is the hallmark of this publication. It
brings together poetry, plays, short stories, humour, old remedies and paintings. The
editor believes that 'experiences which tap the innate abilities to create, evaluate and
appreciate, will help to develop the sensitivity, intelligence, creativity and physical,
moral and social outlook of citizens'. The thirteen plates are photographs of the
paintings entered in the competition and the cover design is a painting by I. Smith.

498 **Reminiscences: creative arts festival.**
Edited by Verna Penn. Road Town, Tortola: Creative Arts Festival
Committee, 1981. 94p.

This is a treasury of award-winning stories and poems; articles on drama, creative
writing, music and photography by eminent local writers; and messages from
concerned authorities. Appendixes include the festival programme and a list of winners
and donors.

# Virgin Islands, US

499 **Dances of our pioneers.**
Grace L. Ryan. Charlotte Amalie, St. Thomas: Public Library, 1972.
66p.

A useful handbook which gives details of early European and other dances which have
influenced the dance forms of the islands.

500 **All in time: a dramatic staged reading of the Emancipation of 1848 and
the Fireburn of 1878, in the Danish West Indies.**
Ruth S. Moore. Charlotte Amalie, St. Thomas: Department of
Cultural Affairs, 1981. 10p.

The author notes that because the history of the islands has been been largely missing
from literature and the history books, that this particular reading seems appropriate,
since 'dramatic staged reading is a forceful and at the same time entertaining method
of reaching the population'. The work was commissioned for 'Emancipation: a second
look' funded by the National Endowment for the Humanities. Schools and non-
profitmaking community groups are urged to read the play whenever possible and to
contribute to the vocal expression of pride in one's history and the struggle for freedom
which it seeks to encourage. The author has written and produced several plays for the
Courtyard Players and other drama groups. She is a freelance writer and part-time
instructor in theatre and speech at the College of the Virgin Islands, St. Croix campus.

501 **Massa Peter.**
Eric Rasmussen, script written by Jorgen Melgaard.    Charlotte
Amalie, St. Thomas: The author, 1976. 12p.

This unusual pamphlet describes the production based on the book *Massa Peter* by
Preben Ramlov, about the famous Danish Governor General of the the Danish West
Indies, Peter von Scholten, and how he lost his honour, post, rank and pension. It tells
of the situation in the islands during the years up to 1848. 'The TV series (in seven
episodes) is a so-called iconographic programme, i.e. stories are read aloud, where the
picture page is composed of drawings'. The drawings, 500 of which tell the story, were
done by Jorn Mathiassen after a research journey to the Virgin Islands in 1974. The
watercolours were also exhibited on St. Croix, United States Virgin Islands on 3 July
1976. The booklet contains some of the paintings and an exciting account of the
project.

# Literature

## Virgin Islands, UK

**502 Boysie and the genips and other stories.**
Jennie Wheatley, edited by Patricia Turnbull, designed by Joseph
Harrigan, illustrated by Joseph Hodge.   St. Lucia: UNESCO, 1983.
32p. (UNDP/Unesco Multi-Island Development series).

A collection of amusing stories which will be of great interest to the reluctant reader
aged twelve to fifteen. The stories centre around Boysie, a young prankster who gets
into trouble once too often. The author and contributors are language teachers at the
British Virgin Islands High School.

**503 A cultural experience: stories and poems.**
Edited by Verna E. Penn.   Road Town, Tortola: Public Library, 1980.
55p.

This collection of award-winning stories and poems submitted to the local Creative
Arts Festival of 1979, embodies the confidence of participants who were encouraged to
explore and express reflections on their own sets of experiences; to recognize the
creative process within themselves and the integrity of their identity. With its
biographical profiles of writers and performers, this anthology is stimulating and
informative.

**504 The hurricane.**
John Levo.   London: Hutchinson, 1930. 288p.

Set in Tortola during the early 20th century, the novel takes us through the struggle
and romance of growing coconut plantations on a Virgin Island . . . and then through
the hell of its devastation by a tropical hurricane.

505   **Jethro and the Jumbie.**
Susan Cooper, illustrated by Ashley Bryan.   New York: Atheneum, 1979. 28p.

Set in the British Virgin Islands, this is the story of how Jethro and the fearsome Jumbie persuaded Jethro's brother, Thomas, to take Jethro deep-sea fishing. Told by the Newberry Award-winning author and illustrated by Ashley Bryan, a widely admired artist with origins in Antigua (Caribbean), it is a funny, warmhearted story. The author, enchanted by the local dialect, has commented: 'they need standard English, but not at the cost of their own bright idiom'. The book is suitable for six- to ten-year-olds but adults would also enjoy its humour.

506   **Johnny Cake Country.**
Verna Penn Moll.   Upton-upon-Severn, England: Mount Sage Press in association with SPA, 1990. 125p. maps.

According to one reviewer, 'this island tale captures the sights, sounds and flavours of the British Virgin Islands. Here one finds the derivation of the word calypso, the origin of johnny cake, the sights, smells and lilt of a West Indian Island interspersed with vignettes from the lives of a diverse group of island residents. These colourful citizens of Johnny Cake Country include Naldo, a young man working for his college tuition; Mr Lettsome, an always on the move taxi driver; Mr Solo, a preacher, who reads symbolism into the word johnny cake, and finally Miss Probsey, who zealously guards the islands' fading customs.' Another reviewer adds: 'the reader may consider this book a priceless treasure relating the strength of a people striving to achieve a place in the sun for themselves and to develop a tourist haven with a preserved legacy of environmental cleanliness'. There are numerous pen-and-ink illustrations by Telpek. It is available in the Caribbean from local bookshops and also from G. Maynard, PO Box 474, East End, Tortola, British Virgin Islands.

507   **Let's take a dip.**
Almein O'Neal, edited by Patricia Turnbull, designed by Joseph Harrigan, illustrated by Ronald Deschamps, Joseph Hodge.   St. Lucia: UNESCO, 1984. 40p. (UNDP/Unesco Multi-Island Development Project series [CAR/83/001]).

The story is set on and around the seas of the British Virgin Islands, an area of the Caribbean hardly explored for young readers. The author's treatment of contemporary themes offers entertainment and will help to stimulate discussion among readers. The training of the twenty-seven specialists from participating islands to develop the project was financed by the Arab Gulf Fund.

508   **Medicine and massage.**
Jennie Wheatley, designed and illustrated by Joan Mallalieu.   Mona, Jamaica: UNESCO, [n.d.]. 6p. (Unesco Multi-Island Project).

This very brief work illustrates the use of local masseurs and local remedies. It is written in a style that will interest reluctant readers.

509 **Now and then.**
Ruby Smith, edited by Patricia Turnbull, designed by Joseph Harrigan,
illustrated by Joseph Hodge. St. Lucia: UNESCO, 1984. 48p.
(UNDP/Unesco Multi-Island Development series).
This work endeavours to bridge the generation gap by skilfully utilizing the
resourcefulness of the older generation as a bountiful repository of history and culture.

510 **Our Virgin Islands.**
Robb White.
Set in the 1930s this is an autobiographical story of a young American couple's
adventures in building a house on Marina Cay, British Virgin Islands. Originally
published by Gollancz in 1955, this work is currently published as *Two on the isle: a
memory of Marina Cay* (New York: Norton, 1985. 185p.).

511 **Virgin Islanders.**
John Levo. London: Hutchinson, 1933. 291p.
The author's observations of the temperament of islanders in the early 20th century are
incorporated in this novel. It pulsates with the manners, behaviour, culture,
expressions and wise sayings of islanders, whom this priest-writer must have studied
intently.

# Poetry

512 **The essence of life and other poems.**
Verna E. Penn. Road Town, Tortola: Caribbean Printing Co., 1976.
17p. map.
There are eighteen poems in this collection of which the reviewers say: 'it captures the
ambiance of those little known but beloved British Virgin Islands . . . she reflects that
special combination of mood, time and place which makes the West Indies unique'.
The work is illustrated; the frontispiece is a painting by local artist, Joseph Hodge, and
the cover illustration is the bell from the historic Church of the Africans at Kingstown,
Tortola, photographed by the architect Paul Wattley.

513 **Reflections: poems.**
Sheila Hyndman. West End, Tortola: The author, 1989. 27p.
A delightful collection of sixteen poems by one of the British Virgin Islands' popular
poets. Sheila's imagery sings the praise of nature's splendour, and conveys deep
feelings for its conservation. She reaches out to something beyond as she pleads for the
protection of her homeland. The wood-cut illustrations, by the well-known artist Roger
Burnett, further enhance this limited first edition of 250 copies. It is available from
local bookshops on the island.

514 **Virgin Verses One: the orginals.**
Quincey Lettsome. Road Town, Tortola: The author, 1969. 76p.
Lettsome's poems are structured in the narrative descriptive style and they speak of the
islands' history and culture.

515 **Virgin Verses Two: selected poems and lyrics.**
Quincey Lettsome. Road Town, Tortola: The author, 1976. 38p.
Some of these are selected from volume one; others were published in the local paper.

516 **Virgin Verses Three: sunlit voices of our destiny.**
Quincey Lettsome. Road Town, Tortola: The author, 1984. 35p.
The author's style matures in this collection which touches on many concerns and aspirations of the islands.

# Virgin Islands, US

517 **Don't stop the carnival.**
Herman Wouk. London: Collins, 1967. 384p.
Set in St. Thomas in the 1950s, the novel depicts scenes and evokes emotions characteristic of the islands' largest corporate cultural endeavour which has taken place in April each year since 1952. Through this work, Wouk has popularized the 'Carnival' on the international scene, particularly throughout the United States of America. One of the main characters of the book, a successful New York Broadway publicity agent gives up the glittering but boring Manhattan life and buys a hotel in this Caribbean island. His adventure involves him with 'bizarre characters and strange ways of the tropic island'. The situations are often explosive and comic, poignant and bitter-sweet, and even when a love-affair ends in heartbreak, 'Carnival is sweet' and nothing can stop it. The novel was first published in 1965.

518 **Kreole ketch n'keep: a collection of West Indian stories.**
Arona Petersen. Charlotte Amalie, St. Thomas: The author, 1975.
104p.
Each of the eight stories in this collection interprets a particular aspect of the social conscience and prevailing value system of the islands. They are humorous, witty and charmingly told by a story-teller whose time has come.

519 **Hugo and his friends.**
Simon Jones-Hendrickson. Frederiksted, St. Croix: Eastern
Caribbean Institute, 1990. 69p.
In this work Hendrickson has personified hurricane Hugo and followed him from his birth to the great devastation which he brought to the islands, St. Croix in particular, in 1989. The hurricane theme runs through both the short story in Part one of the work and through each of the eleven poems in Part two. It is the author's 'contribution to the documentation of the destruction caused by the hurricane'.

520 **Me and my beloved Virgin – St. John.**
Guy H. Benjamin. New York: Benjamin's, 1981. 79p.
Told with great affection and humour, this collection of anecdotes and reminiscences interweaves personal experience with the customs and folklore of the United States

Virgin Islands, thus providing an intimate view of a way of life which is gone forever. The stories revolve around island titles such as hurricanes; Red Cross boxes; courtship and weddings; catching fish; Sunday School picnics; mango trees; and jumbies. There is a glossary and an attractive jacket which was designed by Betty George from a painting by Albert Christian. In recognition of the author's contribution to education in the islands one of the schools was named after him by the Legislature. The book is suitable for all age groups and is available from: Cruz Bay, St. John, PO Box 194, United States Virgin Islands, 00830.

521 **My island: a picture story.**
Lorraine F. Joseph, illustrated by Helen Washington.    St. Croix: CRIC, 1985. 23p. map.
A young student is worried because he does not see his island on the map of the world and when his teacher explains that it is just a dot. He questions everyone in and out of school until at last his brother produces a map of the Virgin Islands for him. The author of the text, an assistant principal of a primary school on St. Croix, writes plays, poems and short stories. This is her first book for children. The illustrator works primarily in oils and exhibits in New York and St. Croix.

522 **Thoughts along the way: Virgin Islands reflections.**
Ariel Melchior.    Charlotte Amalie, St. Thomas: Ariel Melchior, Inc., 1981. 576p.
Ariel Melchior, a printer and co-founder of the *Daily News*, has brought together an anthology of editorials from the *Virgin Islands Daily News*, 1930-78. It begins when 'the world was experiencing the effects of socio-economical upheaval' and concludes with a solemn tribute to a native governor, the late Cyril E. King. The volume admirably expresses the mood of the community. Myron Jackson produced the cover illustration.

523 **Virgin Island commentary.**
Leo Carty.    St. Croix: Virgin Islands Council on the Arts and the National Endowment for the Arts, 1981. 514p.
A vividly illustrated story of the islands told with the pen of a cartoonist.

# Poetry

524 **Bamboula dance and other poems.**
Antonio J. Jarvis.    Charlotte Amalie, St. Thomas: Virgin Islands Art Shop, 1935. 57p.
Personal, warm and enduring, these poems speak of a culture which is simple, but also complex and rich.

525 **I am a man.**
Mao Penha.    Charlotte Amalie, St. Thomas: The author, 1986. 11p.
These eight poems are suitably illustrated and speak of confidence and progress in the islands.

526 **Meditations in solitude.**
Wanda I. Mills. Charlotte Amalie, St. Thomas: Virgin Islands 2000
Organisation, 1989. 56p.

There is much sensitivity and perception in these poems which reflect thought on familiar subjects. The tone is versatile, touching, gentle and uncompromising.

527 **On wings of love and time.**
Clive X. Williams. Frederiksted, St. Croix: Eastern Caribbean
Institute, 1990. 33p.

A young army graduate expresses his concerns about topics such as the genocide of children; the accountability of leaders; and image makers. He performs eloquently on the wings of love and time.

528 **Poems for my son, Paul.**
Isidore Paiewonsky. Charlotte Amalie, St. Thomas: The author,
1981. 93p.

Herman Wouk and Antonio Jarvis provide the introduction to this selection of poems which the author composed in memory of his son who died in a sky-diving accident on 15 October 1967. Each poem is rich in imagery and 'displays a reticent, sensitive spirit and a gift for the exact word . . . is something beautiful.'

529 **Proud of our land and people: a Virgin Islands poetry collection.**
Edited by Jeannette B. Allis, Latifah Lois Chinnery. St. Thomas:
Friends of Enid Baa Library Inc. and the Bureau of Libraries,
Museums and Archaeological Services, 1984. 56p.

A selection from the poems which were submitted for a contest organized by the Library.

530 **Reflections through time.**
Simon B. Jones-Hendrickson. Frederiksted, St. Croix: Eastern
Caribbean Institute, 1989. 54p.

Fifty-two illuminating poems of encouragement for the journey through life from the soul of an economist.

531 **Three islands.**
Vincent O. Cooper, Trevor Parris, Joseph Lisowski. St. Thomas:
University of the Virgin Islands, 1987. 44p.

This collection commemorates the twenty-fifth anniversary of the University of the Virgin Islands. The concept of the anthology emerged from a poetry reading organized by the Humanities Club of the University. All the authors are professors of English at the University of the Virgin Islands.

# Sports and Recreation

## Virgin Islands, UK

532   **Aquatic centres.**
Mark Lawrence.   *Skin Diver*, vol. 36 (March 1987), p. 73-6.
Lawrence locates for the enthusiast all the business concerns which offer aquatic sports and services in the Virgin Islands.

533   **Basic sea skills course.**
Tom Gerker.   *British Virgin Island   Beacon*, vol. 7, no. 43 (18 April 1991), p. 9.
Course organizer, Tom Gerker, a marine businessman, outlines his 'Kids and the sea programme', from which he hopes children will benefit, both recreationally and commercially.

534   **British Virgin Islands Spring Regatta.**
Bill Robinson.   *Yachting*, vol. 160 (July 1986), p. 22-5.
Describes the British Virgin Islands yacht races which end the Caribbean Ocean Racing Triangle series.

535   **First annual philatelic exhibition.**
British Virgin Islands Philatelic Society, with a foreword by Giorgio Migliavacca (Chairman).   Road Town, Tortola: The author, 1990. 36p.
Celebrating the 150th anniversary of the world's first adhesive stamp, the booklet of the exhibition – The One Penny Black 1840-1990 – carries a list of exhibitors and exhibits, a calendar of activities, official messages and articles which should interest stamp enthusiasts. The articles include: 'British Philatelic Society: a profile and a review of two decades of stamp collecting activities'; 'The early postal history of the British Virgin Islands (1702-1866)' by Giorgio Migliavacca; 'The story of the Penny

Black' by Brian Holloway; 'The Leeward Islands stamps' by Marge Doran. Throughout the book there are illustrations of fascinating stamps, for example, the stamp depicting the famous 'missing virgin' dated 1867-70. The exhibition was held on 26-27 May 1990 at Barclays Bank in Road Town, Tortola. Migliavacca who is a stamp enthusiast has written extensively about British Virgin Islands stamps. His articles have appeared in the local newpaper, the *Island Sun*, the *Tourist Handbook* and in several journals. Two of these are: 'The ancient art of rum making celebrated by a new set of stamps', *Island Sun* (20 Aug. 1976) and 'Map and mapmakers on British Virgin Island stamps', *Island Sun* (28 Jan. 1987).

536  **The Royal Mail Steamer *Rhone*: a diving guide and brief history.**
Lauana Mailer.  [n.p.]: Marler, 1978. 76p.
A guide to this famous 19th-century wreck which is also a marine national park and lies off Salt Island, one of the southern British Virgin Islands.

537  **Schooner shoot out.**
Bill Robinson.  *Yachting*, vol. 156 (July 1984), p. 54-6.
Focuses on the race which is an annual feature for classic schooners in the British Virgin Islands. It is brilliantly illustrated.

**British Virgin Islands: territorial report for the year 1987.**
*See* item no. 9.

**Discover.**
*See* item no. 10.

**Social Development Department: annual report for the year 1988.**
*See* item no. 207.

# Virgin Islands, US

538  **Dive guide to the United States Virgin Islands.**
*Skin Diver*, vol. 29 (Jan. 1980), p. 111-28.
Lists and thoroughly describes the dive spots in the United States Virgin Islands.

539  **Hiking in the islands.**
Frances C. Courtsal.  *Sail*, vol. 12 (Nov. 1981), p. 65-70.
An illustrated guide to hiking around the Virgin Islands. Attention is drawn to historic and other places of interest.

540  **Masterpiece in mahogany.**
Vincent Pastena.  *Golf Magazine*, vol. 23 (Jan. 1981), p. 54-7.
A picture of the popular golf course on the island of St. Thomas, United States Virgin Islands is drawn in convincing detail.

541   **United States Virgin Islands: tennis.**
      Roger Cox.   *Tennis*, vol. 19 (Sept. 1983), p. 145-52.
Describes and explains tennis facilities on St. Thomas and encourages visitors and
tourists to try the game while on the island.

**The United States Virgin Islands: a charming blend of American and
Caribbean cultures.**
*See* item no. 16.

**St. John on foot and by car.**
*See* item no. 71.

**St. Thomas on foot and by car.**
*See* item no. 72.

# Libraries, Museums and Archives

## General

542 **Caribbean library development.**
Enid Baa. *Libri*, vol. 20, no. 1-2 (1970), p. 29-34.
The article reiterates some of the problem areas with which Caribbean librarians have struggled in developing libraries and their profession. In it, the author hopes for further achievement through closer regional library co-operation. The paper was presented at the Caribbean Conference on 'Sharing Caribbean resources for study and research', held at the College of the Virgin Islands, St. Thomas, 17-19 March 1969.

543 **Children – protecting their future: a survey of Library Summer/ Outreach Programmes for Children in the Organization of Eastern Caribbean States.**
Cecil Ryan. Castries, St. Lucia: Organization of Eastern Caribbean States in association with the Federal Republic of Germany and the Organization of American States, 1988. 18p. map.
Based on the findings of a survey carried out in the countries of the Eastern Caribbean, including the British Virgin Islands, between 6 and 15 January 1988, the report explains the conceptualization of the survey; its execution; the findings; proposals for new action; prospects for existing programmes and for the Natural Resources Management Project. Six useful appendixes include a directory of potential resource personnel and their particular area of expertise. The general aim of the survey is 'to enhance the position of the Natural Resource Management Programme to assist Public Libraries and volunteer persons to build and maintain an awareness among young people, of the importance of various natural resources to the sustainable development of their countries'. It is a project that has vision and promise.

544 **The role of the Library School in continuing education with special reference to developing countries.**
Daphne Douglas. In: *Association of Caribbean University, Research and Institutional Libraries (ACURIL) 17th Proceedings.* Montreal: University of Montreal, 1987, p. 47-50.
In this paper, the Head of the Library School, University of the West Indies, describes Library School practices, areas of activity, prospects of developing countries and problems in delivering services. The conference was held on St. Croix, 4-10 May 1987.

# Virgin Islands, UK

545 **British Virgin Islands: development of library services.**
Stephen Parker. London: Library Development Consultants for British Virgin Islands Government, 1983. 13p.
The report provides an historical review of the library service, assesses its present impact on society and makes suggestions for a building programme phased to integrate facilities for the archives and museum. Recommendations for staff and training are also included.

546 **Caribbean librarian.**
Pyke Johnson, Jr. *Library Journal* (Feb. 1978), p. 432-4.
In this article, the Managing Editor of Doubleday & Co. – who is also an active Library Board member in Connecticut, United States of America – describes a visit to the British Virgin Islands and the work and activities of the Public Library there.

547 **Information technology and lifelong education for librarians in the Caribbean.**
Peter Moll. In: *Association of Caribbean University, Research and Institutional Libraries (ACURIL) 17th Proceedings.* Montreal: University of Montreal, 1987, p. 112-20.
Moll outlines existing information systems in the region and discusses how libraries and librarians in even the smallest islands could benefit from the 'wave of information technology'. The paper draws a number of illustrations from the author's experience in the British Virgin Islands and also expresses the belief that the Caribbean has comparative advantages which could make the region one of the information centres of the world.

548 **Library Services Department annual report, 1990.**
Road Town, Tortola: Public Library, 1991. 17p.
Reviewing the library services throughout the territory (including Tortola and the outer islands), the report also highlights new services, outreach and extension activities, achievements and developments, staff and training. There are statistics on book stock, membership, library usage and staff. The 1990 report is currently in the press.

# Museums

## Virgin Islands, UK

549 **Projecting images of a past life.**
Sandra Philip. *British Virgin Islands Historical Documents*, vol. 2,
no. 1 (March-April 1985), p. 2-3.
In this brief but vibrant article, the the Assistant Curator explains one of the key roles
of the British Virgin Islands Folk Museum.

## Virgin Islands, US

550 **The story of Fort Christian, 1672.**
Jno. Lightbourn.   Charlotte Amalie, St. Thomas: Bureau of Libraries
and Museums, Department of Conservation and Cultural Affairs, 1973.
22p. bibliog. (Museum leaflet series, no. 1).
Preserved and restored, this building which once served the colony of St. Thomas as
Governor's residence, church, town hall, police station, jail and municipal court, is the
home of the Virgin Islands Museum. The history of the structure is recounted in this
reprint which first apppeared in Walloe's *St. Thomas Almanac and Commercial
Advertiser* of 1881, with a letter by Lightbourn to his son Alberic. There are two plans
of the fort with several references to various community activities which it has served
over the years.

# Archives

## Virgin Islands, UK

551 **A guide to records in the Leeward Islands.**
E.C. Baker.   Oxford: Basil Blackwell for the University of the West
Indies, 1965. 115p.
Baker discusses the state of historical archives in the Leeward Islands group, allocating
a section to each territory. British Virgin Islands records from the 1600s to the 1960s
are catalogued according to form and location. They include records located on
Tortola in the Archive Room (in the Administration Building), the Treasury and the
churches. There is also a brief description of records located in the United Kingdom.
The work is extremely important to researchers in the history of the islands and is also

the initial attempt from which further cataloguing and indexing of archival materials must proceed.

552 **Archives: a resource for national development in a microstate with special reference to the British Virgin Islands.**
Verna E. Penn.   Master's thesis, Loughborough University of Technology, Leicestershire, 1982.

The general background and evolution of the British Virgin Islands as a microstate, are given in Chapters one and two. The main thrust of the work, however, lies in the following chapters: 'Archives in development'; 'Archives in Caribbean microstates'; 'The status of existing information and documentation services'; 'Developing the archives'; and 'Conclusions and recommendations'. Conscious of the microstate's economic, social and political parameters, the thesis develops a flexible plan for appropriate development of the archives of the territory.

553 **A report for the development of the British Virgin Islands Archives.**
Clinton Black.   Kingston, Jamaica: UNESCO for British Virgin Islands Government, 1985. 20p.

Compiled by one of the region's leading archivists, this report assesses the existing state of the territory's archives and makes urgent recommendations for short-, medium- and long-term plans.

# Virgin Islands, US

554 **The historical records of the United States Virgin Islands.**
George F. Tyson.   Charlotte Amalie, St. Thomas: Island Resources Foundation, 1977. 93p.

A report and programme plan, this is the result of a survey of West Indian materials in the Copenhagen Royal Archives. The report makes five important recommendations for the development of a Territorial Archive in the United States Virgin Islands.

**Preservation of the Sephardic records of the island of St. Thomas, Virgin Islands.**
*See* item no. 194.

**The historical context of medical practice in the Virgin Islands.**
*See* item no. 219.

# Books and Publishing

555 **Book production in the British Virgin Islands.**
Reginald D. Payne.   Road Town, Tortola: British Development in the
Caribbean for British Virgin Islands Government, 1977. 13p.

Payne presents the case for the installation of a low-cost book production print unit to
be housed either at the Public library or at the Education Department. The regional
adviser based his proposal on developments at a seminar/workshop for teachers,
librarians and educators, held earlier in the year. Six useful appendixes describe the
technical components for operating the proposed unit.

# Mass Media

## General

**556 Caribbean media directory.**
Compiled and edited by Joseph McPherson.   Kingston, Jamaica:
Jamaica Institute of Political Education, Eastern Caribbean Institute
for Democracy, 1986. 64p. map.
Provides a list of media enterprises in operation in the territories of the English-
speaking Caribbean. It also gives brief information on geography, people, politics,
government and economic activities.

## Virgin Islands, UK

**557 The British Virgin Island Beacon.**
Road Town, Tortola: L.M. Abbott, 1988- . weekly.
Published on Thursdays, the paper carries general news and accommodates a wide
range of opinion.

**558 Island Sun.**
Road Town, Tortola: Sun Enterprises (BVI) Ltd, 1962- . twice weekly.
Founded by Carlos Downing, the paper carries general news, features and government
releases.

559 **Limin' Times.**
Road Town, Tortola: Island Publishing Services, 8 Sept. 1988- . weekly.
An entertainment magazine and guide to the happenings in the islands. It was published earlier as 'TV Guide Weekly' and as 'This week in the BVIs'.

560 **Torch.**
Road Town, Tortola: Social Welfare Council, April 1948-1957.
monthly.
The newsletter of the Social Welfare Council, this publication also carried general news items and served as the only newspaper for the entire country in the 1940s and 1950s. It is today a valuable reference source for an insight into the socio-economic condition of the territory almost fifty years ago.

561 **Tortola Times.**
Road Town, Tortola: Norman Fowler, 1959-61. weekly.
Succeeded by the *Island Sun*.

562 **The welcome: tourist guide.**
Road Town, Tortola: Island Publishing Services in collaboration with the British Virgin Islands Tourist Board and the Hotel and Commerce Association, *c.*1970- . bi-monthly.
A well-prepared guide for tourists consisting of substantial articles on island developments, information on accommodation, shopping, work permits, cruising permits, taxes, doctors, and other information invaluable to visitors. The guide was established in 1973 as *The BVIslander*; in 1974 the title changed to *Virgin Islander*. The current title dates from the early 1980s.

# Virgin Islands, US

563 **Daily News.**
Charlotte Amalie, St. Thomas: Ariel Melchior, Jr, 1930- . daily.
Publishes general news.

564 **St. Croix Avis.**
Christiansted, St. Croix: Brodhurst's Printery, 1844- . daily.
Carries general news and substantial articles on topical issues.

565 **Pride.**
Charlotte Amalie, St. Thomas: Virgin Island Guide Printing and Publishing Company, 1982- . monthly.
This news magazine covers vital issues that affect the islands and their people. The articles, which are mostly exclusive, are fresh and concise, representing well the dynamic community the magazine serves.

# Professional Journals

## General

**566  Journal of Caribbean Studies.**
Coral Gables, Florida: Association of Caribbean Studies, 1981- . twice yearly.

Publishes scholarly articles on all aspects of Caribbean studies including anthropology, the arts, economics, education, folk culture, geography, history, languages, literature, music, politics, religion and sociology. Several editions carry articles on both groups of Virgin Islands. Some of these topics are also covered in *Infonet Current Awareness Bulletin* (Castries, St. Lucia: Organization of Eastern Caribbean States, 1987- . monthly) which lists the output of the regional database and covers economics, agriculture, trade, industry, tourism, natural resources, health, education, law and international relations. British Virgin Islands items are included and should interest policy-makers, planners, and technical and administrative personnel in the public and private sectors. Two regional journals of more specialized content are: *Canto: Quarterly Review of the Caribbean Association of National Telecommunication Organizations* (Port of Spain, Trinidad: Caribbean Association of National Telecommunication Organizations, [1984?]- . quarterly) which informs members of technological and administrative developments taking place in the organizations of the Association. It aims to reach policy-makers of the Caribbean to sharpen their awareness of these developments and it reaches out internationally, with news, information and analysis of telecommunication developments in/or affecting the Caribbean. And *CEIS (Caribbean Energy Information System) Update* (Kingston, Jamaica: Scientific Research Council, 1967- . quarterly) which provides an update on the activities at the regional and national focal points of the CEIS – a co-operative networking system committed to the sharing and exchange of information in support of regional energy activities – and lists researchers, by country, with representation from the United States Virgin Islands. The British Virgin Islands is one of the twelve founding participating countries.

567 **Caribbean Insight.**
London: West India Committee, 1977- . monthly.
A monthly news and economic magazine, covering thirty-five countries in the Caribbean and Central America. There are frequent news updates on the politics, facts and figures of economic developments and business projects of individual islands, including the British Virgin Islands and, less frequently, the United States Virgin Islands.

568 **Caribbean Update.**
Maplewood, New Jersey: Kal Wagenheim, 1985- . monthly.
Focuses on economic and related news of interest to business and government executives, journalists and scholars. Statistics are updated and individual islands are represented.

569 **Organization of Eastern Caribbean States – Natural Resources Management Project: News one.**
Castries, St. Lucia: Organization of Eastern Caribbean States, Natural Resources Management Project, 1987- . irregular.
The newsletter of the Organization's Natural Resources Management Project giving information and news about on-going and future activities. It also lists publications to date.

# Virgin Islands, UK

570 **Island Accents.**
Road Town, Tortola: Sunflower Productions, 1988- . quarterly.
This is the business magazine of the islands, produced in full colour. It emphasizes business and consumer promotions, and offers profiles of successful businesses and persons. First launched on World Literacy Day by Sandra Philip, the magazine provides an attractive visual presentation of the people of the islands. It is available from: Sunflower Productions, PO Box 270, Road Town, Tortola, British Virgin Islands.

571 **Newsletter of the British Virgin Islands Hotel and Commerce Association.**
Road Town, Tortola: British Virgin Islands Hotel and Commerce Association, [1990?]- . quarterly.
Carries news of changes within the Association, for example, election news or proceedings of the annual general meeting. The Association's involvement and activities in the community are also noted, for example, its contribution to annual regattas, and to creating an employee assistance programme.

572   **The Resource.**
Road Town, Tortola: Aaronrod Communication Ltd., British Virgin
Islands National Parks Trust, British Virgin Islands Tourist Board and
Eastern Caribbean Natural Resources and Management Programme
(ECNRMP), 1983- . quarterly.
Deals with conservation and development issues in the British Virgin Islands.
However, the last issue to date is July-Sept. 1988.

573   **Trust News.**
Road Town, Tortola: Friends of the National Parks Trust, 1986- .
quarterly.
An invaluable forum for 'green' issues which provides information about the activities
of Trust projects, ranging from current environmental education, park improvements
and wildlife protection to ventures planned for the future. The well-illustrated articles,
though brief, are the work of knowledgeable writers.

574   **Virgin Islands Historical Documents.**
Road Town, Tortola: Public Library, Ministry of Health, Education
and Welfare, 1985- . quarterly.
Attractively produced, this little periodical carries brief but well-researched historical
and cultural articles by leading historians and members of the Library Staff. Founded
by V.P. Moll, it is now edited by librarian Bernadine Louis.

# Virgin Islands, US

575   **Caribbean Writer.**
Charlotte Amalie, St. Thomas: Caribbean Research Institute, 1987- .
annual.
A literary magazine which offers publishing opportunities for Caribbean-based writers
and encourages the creation of quality poetry and fiction in the Virgin Islands and
throughout the region. It is available locally from CRI, University of the Virgin
Islands, PO Box 10,000, Kingshill, St. Croix, Virgin Islands 00850, and also from
regional and international booksellers.

576   **Economic Review.**
Charlotte Amalie, St. Thomas: Virgin Islands Department of
Commerce, Office of Policy Planning and Research, 1977- . semi-
annual.
Publishes articles and statistics pertaining to the economy, knowledge of which is
essential for developmental planning in both the public and private sectors.

577 **Farm Management Factsheet.**
Charlotte Amalie, St. Thomas: Cooperative Extension Service, College
of the Virgin Islands, 1984- . irregular.
Carries articles on the methods and processes of the essentials of farm financial
management. 'Depreciation Methods' are explained in Factsheet no. 2, for example.

578 **Fish and Wildlife News.**
Charlotte Amalie, St. Thomas: Virgin Islands Bureau of Wildlife,
1972- . quarterly.
A newsletter about the activities, projects and research findings of the Bureau.

579 **Foundation News.**
Charlotte Amalie, St. Thomas: Islands Resources Foundation, 1972- .
irregular.
Carries news and reviews of the Foundation's projects and publications.

580 **Government Information Service Bulletin.**
Charlotte Amalie, St. Thomas: United States Virgin Islands
Government, 1978- . monthly.
Carries mainly news of the Government's plans and programmes.

581 **Information.**
Charlotte Amalie, St. Thomas: Virgin Islands Bureau of Libraries and
Museums, 1976- .
News about the activities, services and plans of the libraries and museums in the
United States Virgin Islands.

582 **Journal of the College of the Virgin Islands.**
Charlotte Amalie, St. Thomas: College of the Virgin Islands, 1975- .
irregular.
Carries articles on the various disciplines studied at the University as well as important
topical local and regional issues. (The College achieved University status in 1986.)

583 **News and Views.**
Charlotte Amalie, St. Thomas: Chamber of Commerce, 1978- .
iregular.
Covers St. Thomas and St. John and informs its members of business and trade
opportunites via announcements of, for example, local, regional and international
seminars, trade conventions and emporia.

584 **Social Sciences Newsletter.**
Charlotte Amalie, St. Thomas: Division of Social Services, College of
the Virgin Islands, 1980- . irregular.
Exists to disseminate information from the various components of the Division, about
new knowledge and challenges, projects and prospects.

585 **St. Croix Chamber of Commerce Newsletter.**
Christiansted, St. Croix: St. Croix Chamber of Commerce Newsletter,
1963- . irregular.
Serves its members on St. Croix by keeping them informed of news and happenings in
the commercial world. It also records the association's endeavours, meetings and
proceedings.

586 **St. Croix Landmarks Society.**
Christiansted, St. Croix: St. Croix Landmarks Society, 1971- .
Carries news of the Society's special educational and restoration projects and uses its
pages to increase the community's awareness of local history.

587 **St. Thomas this Week.**
St. Thomas: Margot Bachman, 1959- . weekly.
Covering business and tourist information, the booklet is distributed to hotels, travel
agencies and other sectors of the tourist industry.

588 **Graduate Bulletin.**
Charlotte Amalie, St. Thomas: University of the Virgin Islands, 1991- .
annual.
All matters relating to the graduate programme of the University of the Virgin Islands
are dealt with. There are explanations of graduate education, general admission
requirements, admission procedures, student classification, senior citizen education
programmes, rules and regulations, and descriptions of theses, tuition and courses. It is
the medium used to update the local and external community about what the
University has to offer.

589 **Virgin Islands Archaeological Society Journal.**
Charlotte Amalie, St. Thomas: Archaeological Society, 1974- . semi-
annual.
Published to record the results of expeditions, digs and studies of archaeological sites,
architecture, artefacts etc., and to encourage discussion, debate and further research
and development.

590 **Virgin Islands Education Review.**
Charlotte Amalie, St. Thomas: Office of Public Information,
Department of Education, 1981- . irregular.
Carries educational issues and topics by scholars and teachers. It also publishes book
reviews and the results of tests and surveys carried out by the Department.

591 **Virgin Islands Employment Security Agency Bulletin.**
Charlotte Amalie, St. Thomas: Department of Labour, 1982- .
quarterly.
Seeks to inform on matters pertaining to work situations, for example, regulations
affecting employees' hours of work, contracts, benefits, etc.

592    **Virgin Islands Labour Market Review.**
       Charlotte Amalie, St. Thomas: [n.p.], 1978- . irregular.
A newsletter of labour market activity largely presented in tables, graphs, figures and drawings.

593    **The Virgin Islands Voice: the International Caribbean Magazine.**
       Charlotte Amalie, St. Thomas: The Virgin Islands Voice, 1989- .
       quarterly.
Publishes general articles about sport, fashion, politics and issues affecting the Caribbean.

# School magazines

594    **Straight From Us.**
       Road Town, Tortola: British Virgin Islands High School, [1970s]- .
       irregular.
The magazine of the British Virgin Islands High School is published periodically and carries articles mainly researched by the students. An entire issue is sometimes devoted to one theme; for example, vol. 2, no. 1: 'Looks at sugarcane in the British Virgin Islands' and vol. 2, no. 2: 'Looks at the sea'. The articles are usually aptly illustrated by students in the art department.

595    **Glimpses.**
       Charlotte Amalie, St. Thomas: Charlotte Amalie High School, 1981- .
       irregular.
The literary magazine of the Charlotte Amalie High School carries poems, stories, cartoons, essays and illustrations. It is funded by the Virgin Islands Council on the Arts and the Hess Oil Virgin Islands Corporation.

# Encyclopaedias and Directories

**596 Agricultural research directory.**
Robert Webb, Walter Knansenberger, Houston Holder. St. Thomas: College of the Virgin Islands Eastern Caribbean Centre, 1986. 98p.

An alphabetical listing of organizations and individuals involved in agricultural research and development in Eastern (and other regionally selected) Caribbean countries. Entries for both the British and United States Virgin Islands are included.

**597 British Virgin Islands telephone directory.**
Road Town, Tortola: Cable and Wireless West Indies Ltd, 1991. 48p.

An alphabetical listing of telephone, facsimile and telex numbers for 1991-92. There are special listings for services, government departments and yellow pages. The cover illustration shows the recently installed card and coin booths in operation.

**598 British Virgin Islands tourism directory.**
Road Town, Tortola: British Virgins Islands Tourist Board, 1989- . irregular.

Journalistic articles by notable writers describe geographical and historical aspects. It provides information on air communications to and from the islands, taxi rates, car rentals, sight-seeing tours, hotel and guesthouse rates, sailing and water sports, marinas, sailing schools, diving tours/underwater photography, customs and duties.

**599 Directory of human services.**
Charlotte Amalie, St. Thomas: Department of Human Services, 1988. 41p.

The contents of this work are arranged under two headings: 'Services offered by the Department of Human Services' and 'Services offered by other agencies'. In the first instance they include services for adults; children, youth and families; senior citizens; services dealing with disabilities and rehabilitation; and volunteers and special programmes. In the second instance the services include miscellaneous ones; those from Virgin Islands churches; social and leisure projects; and federal programmes and agencies. Names and addresses of facilities and resource personnel are given.

**600 Virgin Islands government directory.**
Charlotte Amalie, St. Thomas: Bureau of Public Administration, 1983. 62p.

Lists offices, departments, judiciary and agencies giving names of officers, addresses and telephone numbers.

**601 Virgin Islands of the United States: Blue Book.**
Edited by Jeannette B. Allis, foreword by Henry C. Chang. Charlotte Amalie, St. Thomas: Bureau of Libraries, Museums and Archaeological Services, 1983. 100p.

First published in 1981, this is a valuable guide to the government of the Virgin Islands. There is information on the flag, territorial bird [Yellow breast, *Coreba flaveola*] and flower [Yellow elder, *Tacoma stans*], the Virgin Islands March and significant political events. The names of officers, addresses and functions of offices and departments – executive, judiciary, commissions and agencies. Lists of labour, community and religious organizations, and of libraries and schools, are comprehensive in coverage. A detailed description of the legislature with historical background, and a promise that the guide will be revised bi-annually, make this a very reliable source. Other members of the publication committee are: Kathy Gregg, Delores Jowers, Helen Lawrence and Elizabeth K. Rogers.

**602 University of the Virgin Islands catalogue, 1991-92.**
Charlotte Amalie, St. Thomas: University of the Virgin Islands, 1991. 177p. map.

Presenting a very up-to-date image of the University, the catalogue states the mission of the University, and lists the members of the Board of Trustees, Board of Overseers, Faculty and professional staff. It also describes in detail each of its three campuses, student services, the cost of tutition and the courses the University offers. There is a brief history of the University and the academic calendar for each of the campuses is outlined. The catalogue is illustrated with pictures of university personnel, students and activities.

# Bibliographies and Abstracts

## General

**603  Cagrindex: abstracts of the agricultural literature of the Caribbean.**
St. Augustine, Trinidad and Tobago: Main Library, University of the
West Indies. quarterly
Covers agriculture, agricultural education, and literature surveys of the general
Caribbean region and also of specific islands.

**604  Carindex: social sciences and the humanities.**
St. Augustine, Trinidad: University of the West Indies, 1977- .
Indexes published works and significant articles relating to Caribbean social sciences
and the humanities. A list of periodicals and newpapers indexed is given and although
only few entries appear for the Virgin Islands, they are usually significant references.

**605  Complete Caribbeana, 1900-1975: a bibliographical guide to scholarly
literature, 4 vols.**
Lambros Comitas.    Milwood, NY: KTO Press, 1977.
An established bibliographical source for Caribbean material published in the 19th and
20th centuries, this guide is arranged in subject categories in each of which the entries
are alphabetically arranged. It lists over two hundred items relating to the Virgin
Islands under the headings: the Leeward Islands; Virgin Islands; and under each
individual island, for example, St. Thomas; St. Croix; Tortola. It updates *A topical
bibliography*, also by Comitas and first published in 1968.

606 **Theses on Caribbean topics, 1778-1968.**
Enid M. Baa. San Juan, Puerto Rico: University of Puerto Rico Press, for the Institute of Caribbean Studies, 1970. 141p.

A total of 1,242 doctoral dissertations, master's and other theses covering the entire Caribbean are listed. Indexes to the main alphabetical sequence are arranged by university, country studied, subject and chronology. It is a useful checklist for all those whose research interests are directly or indirectly linked to the Caribbean region.

# Virgin Islands, UK

607 **Current Awareness Bulletin.**
Road Town, Tortola: Documentation Centre, Library Services Department, 1989- . quarterly.

The serial lists the output of the Centre's database and should be of interest to policymakers, planners, technical and administrative personnel in government and public sectors.

608 **Government reports.**
V.E. Penn. Road Town, Tortola: Public Library, Ministry of Social Services, 1981. 113p.

A list of government publications including reports located in the Public Library and other collections within the territory. Cumulative indexes of catalogues issued in 1975 and 1979 are also incorporated.

# Virgin Islands, US

609 **A bibliography of articles on the Danish West Indies and the United States Virgin Islands in the *New York Times*, 1867-1975.**
Edited and compiled by Arnold Highfield in collaboration with Max Bumgarner. Gainesville, Florida: Centre for Latin American Studies and University Presses of Florida for the Caribbean Research Institute, 1978. 209p.

Each of the 1,054 chronologically arranged entries gives the title, author, date and pagination of an article.

610 **Bibliography of the Virgin Islands of the United States.**
Charles Frederick Reid. New York: H.W. Wilson, 1941. 225p.

A very useful work which covers early published materials up to 1940. It was prepared with the assistance of the Federal Works Agency, Works Project Administration for the City of New York, Division of Community Service Programme.

611 **Caribbeana.**
Virgin Islands Libraries Network (VILNET). Charlotte Amalie, St.
Thomas: Bureau of Libraries, Museums and Archaeological Services,
1979- . quarterly.

A useful list of recent acquisitions of Caribbean materials in libraries in the United
States Virgin Islands.

612 **Union List of periodicals and newspapers in the United States Virgin
Islands libraries.**
Charlotte Amalie, St. Thomas: Division of Libraries, Museums and
Archaeological Services, 1984- .

Shows the holdings of periodicals and newspapers for all public libraries on St.
Thomas, St. Croix and St. John.

613 **The Virgin Islands ecosystem.**
St. Thomas: Caribbean Research Institute, 1968. 4p.

A bibliography of ecological materials available at the Virgin Islands Ecological
Research Station at Lameshur Bay, St. John. It will be useful to anyone studying the
ecology of the Virgin Islands and the region.

614 **The Virgin Islands of the United States in periodical literature.**
Robert V. Vaughn. Christiansted, St. Croix: Aye-Aye Press, 1974.

A bibliography of social, economic and political conditions referred to in recent
periodical literature. The primary emphasis is on Virgin Islands newspapers for 1973
and minor references back to 1966.

**Selected bibliography of materials and resources on women in the
Caribbean . . .**
*See* item no. 230.

# Index of Authors and Titles

## Virgin Islands, UK

178

Fleming, Stewart 287
*Flora and fauna of the*
  *Caribbean* 84
*Folklore of the British*
  *Virgin Islands* 179
Fones, John Scott 166
*Food and nutrition*
  *education: a guide for*
  *college tutors in the*
  *English-speaking*
  *Caribbean* 427
Forbes, Alexander C. 50
*Forestry in the Leeward*
  *Islands: the British*
  *Virgin Islands* 359
Fountain, Ellen 470
*Four flakes of rust: a study*
  *of the Long Bay*
  *cannon, part one* 404
*Four flakes revisited: a*
  *consideration of the*
  *Long Bay cannon,*
  *part two* 405
Fowler, Norman 561
Frank Knight and Rutley
  390
Fraser, B. 381
*From Columbus to Castro:*
  *the history of the*
  *Caribbean 1492-1969*
  111

G

Gallagher, Rodney 296
Gaume, Martine 392
*General orders for the*
  *Public Service of the*
  *British Virgin Islands*
  271
Geoghegan, Tighe 387, 412
*Geographical distribution*
  *of the ciguatoxic fish in*
  *the eastern half of the*
  *British Virgin Islands*
  369
Geography for C.X.C. 18
*Geopolitics of the*
  *Caribbean: ministates*
  *in a wider world* 19
George, Aubrey 222
Georges, Elton 79

Georges, R. 221-2
Gerker, Tom 534
Gladfelter, Elizabeth 481
Glasgow, E. 142
Glazier, Stephen 159
Gonzales, Edward 236
Goodwin, Melvin H. 367
Gorgon, D. J. 28
Government Information
  Office 26, 316, 318,
  324, 488
Government of the British
  Virgin Islands 316
*Government reports* 608
Greenaway, Dean 474
Greenberg, Idaz 98, 101
Greenspan, Bernard 38
*Growth of the modern West*
  *Indies* 112
Grundy, Milton 301
*Guide to corals and fishes*
  *of Florida, the*
  *Bahamas and the*
  *Caribbean* 101
*Guide to records in the*
  *Leeward Islands* 551
Gupta, S. Sen 331
Gurney, J. J. 54

H

Hargreaves, Dorothy and
  Bob 87
Harrigan, Joseph 450, 502,
  507, 509
Harrigan, Norwell 25, 119,
  126, 139, 142, 201,
  222, 243, 247, 252,
  254, 285, 435, 450,
  457, 502
*Health and social aspects of*
  *child development for*
  *nurses, teachers and*
  *parents* 217
Heine, Jorge 236
Hepburn, Doris Farrington
  447
*Herbarium of the Virgin*
  *Islands National Park*
  483
Herdman, J. M. A. 10,
  242, 273

*Higher education in a*
  *micro-state: a theory*
  *of the Raran society*
  457
Highfield, Arnold 8
*Historical account of the*
  *Virgin Islands in the*
  *West Indies* 114
*Historical context of*
  *medical practice in the*
  *British Virgin Islands*
  219
*History of the British West*
  *Indies* 113
*History of the Virgin*
  *Islands, 1672 to 1970*
  122
*History, civil and*
  *commercial of the*
  *British colonies in the*
  *West Indies* 115
Hodge, Calvin 450
Hodge, I. 142
Hodge, Joseph 502, 507,
  509, 512
Holder, Houston 596
Holloway, B. 535
Holloway, B. P. 94
Hotel and Commerce
  Association 562
*Housing programmes and*
  *policies in the British*
  *Virgin Islands: a*
  *perspective for*
  *twenty-eight years*
  *(1973-2000)* 393
*How to retire to the*
  *Caribbean* 12
Howard, James 26
Howell, Christopher 78,
  384
*Human resources*
  *development planning*
  379
Hunt, Sydney 12
Hunte, George 7
*Hurricane* 504
*Hurricanes in paradise,*
  *perception and reality*
  *of the hurricane*
  *hazard in the Virgin*
  *Islands* 38
*Hurricanes: their nature*
  *and history, especially*

# Index of Subjects

## Virgin Islands, UK

### A

Abolition *see*
  Emancipation
Abolition Act 1833 139
Accommodation 3
Accounts 302
Administration and Local
  Government 270-2
Administration building,
  Anegada 240
African languages 170
Afro-Caribbean
  community 241
Agriculture and fisheries
  289, 340-70
  *see also* Farms; History;
  Land usage; Fruits
Airlines
  *see also* Transport and
  communications
Airports 41, 46
Amphibians 92, 96
Anchorages 48, 51, 388
  *see also names of
  individual anchorages*
Anegada 24, 41, 58, 99
Anegada Development
  Corporation 285
Anegada Horseshoe Reef
  398
Anegada, data atlas 417
  economic stagnation 285
  fauna 92, 99
  feudal development 285
  reefs (chart) 24
  tales 179
  wrecks 24, 404
Anglican Church, transfer
  184
Anglo-Caribbean societies
  197
  culture 197
Anniversary 186
Antigua 400

Annual information 6
Anthropology 104, 159
  problems
    archaeological 104
    economic 104
    ethnological 104
    sociological 104
  *Homo caribensis* 104
Arawaks
  bowls, tools 103
  culture, games 103, 105
  religion 103
  sculpture 103
  sites 103
Archaeology 103-6
  archaeological survey
    105
  conch shells moulds 105
  Indian spindle whorl 105
  Indians, origins 103
  International
    Association for
    Caribbean
    Archaeology 106
  Mongoloid archaic
    peoples 106
  petroglyphs 103
  pre-history 106
  prehistoric animals 106
  Saladero 103
  Virgin Islands 106
  zemis 103
  *see also* Arawaks
Architecture 392-4
  architectural styles 394
  *see also* Conservation;
  History
Art, regional 21
  *see also* Folklore;
  History
Arts and crafts 7
Assets and liabilities 298
Atlases *see* Maps and
  atlases
Auditor, statutory duties
  302

Autonomy 141

### B

Bahamas 49, 98, 101
Banks and banking 2, 279,
  296
  licensing 296
Banking business,
  regulations 319
Bareboat industry 10, 49,
  321
Bay rum plant 328
Beaches 46
  development 419
Beef Island 41, 58
Biannual reports 9
Bibliography 603-8
  *see also individual
  subjects e.g. Tourism*
Biological survey 99
Birds 92-4
  characteristics 90, 94
  identification guide 90,
    93-4
  locations 90
Births 283
Boat-builders 142
Boating industry 320-3,
  326
  *see also* Sports and
  recreation
Botanic gardens
  Christmas garden 410
  cottage museum 410
  *Heliconia* collection 410

187

# Index of Authors and Titles

## Virgin Islands, US

(Please refer to the Virgin Islands, UK index for general authors and titles not indexed here.)

197

# Index of Subjects

## Virgin Islands, US

(Please refer to the Virgin Islands, UK index for general topics not indexed here.)

205

209

# Maps of the Virgin Islands

The maps overleaf show the more important towns and other features.

# Maps: British Virgin Islands

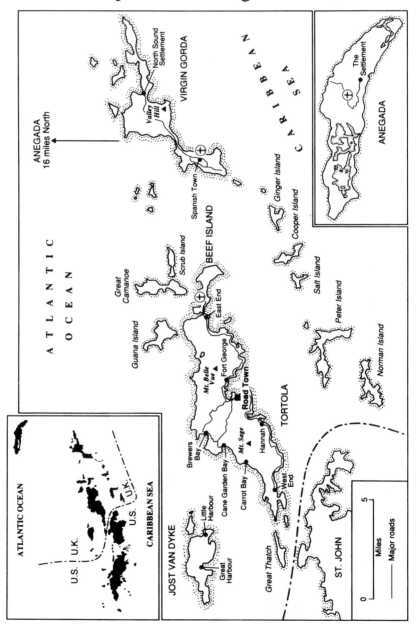

# United States Virgin Islands

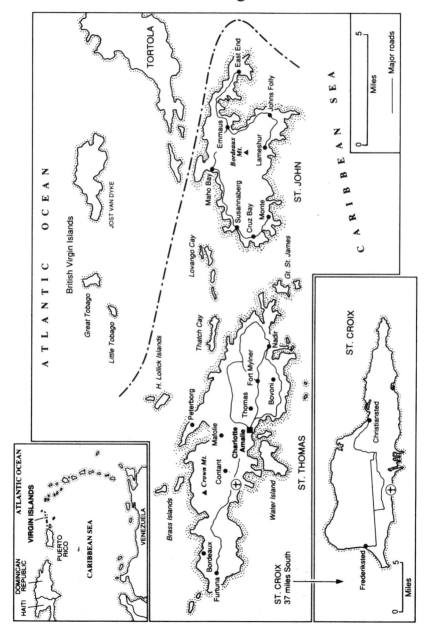